A DOCTOR LOOKS
AT WAR

A DOCTOR LOOKS AT WAR

MY YEAR IN IRAQ

Michael C. Hodges, M.D.

Tate Publishing *& Enterprises*

TATE PUBLISHING
        & Enterprises

Published in the United States of America

ISBN: 1–5988659–4–3
06.12.1

*This book is dedicated to my wife, Ana, and my three children –
Noah, Logan and Caroline. They are the most important people on earth
to me. In my opinion, they are the heroes who receive the least credit
because they are left behind to try to maintain normalcy while their
loved ones go away to war.*

Ana, you're the one who enables me to be the man that I am.

Table of Contents

Foreword

The highest compliment one soldier can give another is to say they would go to war with you. *A Doctor Looks At War* provides a rare, uncut version of one man's journey at the beginning of Operation Iraqi Freedom. The thoughts, actions, and stories that lie within this book capture the essence of war, from a medical perspective. Michael Hodges describes his professional world of saving lives in a war zone, while giving the reader an incredible picture of what a Christian emotionally, mentally, physically, and spiritually goes through in the unique environment of war. Every individual will be able to relate to something that is written. There will be moments of laughter and of tears mixed with episodes of anger.

Michael Hodges started the war as a trained physician, but an inexperienced soldier. His journey takes him far from his family and his comfort zone into an arena of fear, deprivation and loneliness. His faith grounds him and provides the basis he needs to survive his experience in the war zone.

I have gone to war with Mike Hodges once, and I would go with him again! His openness and his vulnerability is refreshing. This book is much more than a journal. It is a detailed history of the 28th Combat Support Hospital's (28th CSH's) first deployment in support of the Global War On Terrorism. It describes issues of faith, love, death and dying, and the life-sustaining work and relationships of the 28th CSH. I would recommend this book to all readers, military or civilian, Christian or not. The insights found in this book will traverse all boundaries to the human beneath, a journey through the realities of war from one man's perspective.

Keith N. Croom
Group Chaplain
1st Special Warfare Training Group (Airborne)

Author's Note

This story is the condensed version of the journal that I kept while deployed in Iraq with the 28th Combat Support Hospital from Fort Bragg, North Carolina. The early chapters were often written after the events had occurred because I had limited access to electricity for my laptop computer and because I wanted to avoid excessive exposure of my laptop to the blowing sand. Other entries were written as our experiences happened. Times are listed in military time that uses a continuous 24-hour clock running from 1 to 24 and then resets. For instance, 1400 hours is the same as twelve o'clock plus two hours, or 2 PM. All entries are written from my perspective and reflect only my opinions.

1 / Introduction

Even though I'd been a physician in the Army for many years, I had never faced the issue of having to go to war. In December 2002, my department boss was hearing more and more rumors that the 28th Combat Support Hospital (CSH) from Fort Bragg, North Carolina, would be used in the medical effort for any military action that occurred. The talk of war had been building for many months both in the military and in the community at large, but this marked the first time that I seriously considered that the war would directly impact me.

I'd been assigned as a fill-in physician to this combat hospital in the summer of 2002. In peacetime, most physicians in the Army work at established medical facilities and hospitals providing care for soldiers, family members, and retirees. There are only a few physicians assigned directly to the war-fighting units. In situations of deployment, the war-fighting units are assigned physicians like me from the medical facilities to accompany them and provide the healthcare mission. This task is accomplished through the Professional Filler System (PROFIS) and includes physicians, nurses, and other healthcare providers like physician assistants and nurse practitioners.

A combat support hospital is potentially a 296-bed facility that is set up to provide pharmacy, laboratory, radiology, and surgery services on the battlefield. The facility is built from a combination of canvas tents that are connected to hard-sided boxes that house the areas that need more sterile control such as the laboratory, radiology, and the operating rooms. This hospital – when fully erected – requires a land area of as much as 25 acres and has a total staff of over five hundred soldiers, roughly thirty of whom are physicians.

I came to be a physician in the Army by way of a Health Professions Scholarship that I had accepted in 1988 to finance my medical school education. After residency training in Fort Bliss, Texas, and fellowship training in Fort Sam Houston, Texas, my family and I moved to Fayetteville, North Carolina, in the summer of 2000 for my assignment as a cardiologist at Womack Army Medical Center (WAMC). By this time my wife Ana – who I'd met in the scholarship program – had fulfilled her obligation and had left the Army for a part-time practice with a pediatrics group in Fayetteville.

Fort Bragg is an Army installation that has a very high operational tempo, and physicians are in short supply for the assignments. When news of my PROFIS assignment to the 28th CSH came in late summer 2002, I was concerned about the deployment issue, but at that time it did not present as an immediate threat.

During our years in training my wife and I had started a family, and we had three small children – aged 3, 5, and 7 years old – and I was worried about the impact on them of me being deployed. I am not implying that I was in a unique position as a military father who faces deployment, but I had yet to face an actual period of time away from them, despite being on active duty for several years. At the time of my assignment, the 28th CSH was just completing a rotation in the Balkans, and I thought that it was unlikely the hospital would be tasked again so soon. There was no significant talk of war with Iraq, and my concerns quickly faded into the background.

By the time we heard of the possibility of deployment, I still had hopes that a peaceful solution would be found in Iraq. We proceeded with our plans and went to Fort Lauderdale for Christmas to visit with my wife's family. Their reaction to my possible deployment was far stronger than expected. Even though they knew that I wore the uniform and worked each day in an Army hospital, I don't think they'd ever allowed for the idea that I might be someday called to go. The mood amongst our family members and friends was quite unlike any prior holiday together.

By mid-January the rumors had acquired substance, and we all began to make definite plans for the inevitable. We were ordered to begin the Anthrax vaccination series and to receive the Smallpox vaccine. In the second week of February, we received orders to report for duty to the 28th CSH, effective on the sixteenth.

As our training and preparation progressed, I was introduced to the side of the Army that I really didn't know having spent my career in hospitals. I was thrust into the full-scale world of completing forms and standing in endless lines for things that we didn't need in the first place or to be told that we'd completed the paperwork incorrectly or were in the wrong place. I was also fully immersed into the world of Army training exercises that attempted to prepare us for any sort of military scenario we might encounter, such as being attacked by biological or chemical agents or having to construct our tent hospital wearing our chemical protection suits. We spent a great deal of time with the protective masks and practiced putting them on quickly and safely. We then conducted exercises where we were exposed to tear gas to make sure that our masks were properly sealed and working. And we went to the firing range to qualify using our weapons.

Altogether we spent the next several days training to deploy and the healthcare aspect of the mission was rarely mentioned. At times I found myself slipping into the world of thinking like a soldier and forgetting my skills as a physician. At the end of the training there were no formal deployment orders providing us a date to depart, and so we were released for a few days. Those who had left their families to come to Ft Bragg were able to go home. Our break lasted only a few days as we were re-called late in the first week of March, and the preparations increased in intensity.

On the night before we departed – which we didn't realize at the time because we'd just been told to be ready over the next few days – my good friend Bill D. and I took our wives out for a nice dinner to spend an evening away from the children and to catch up on old times. It turned out to be the last meal before we would leave, and I'll always recall it fondly because of the relaxed atmosphere and the fellowship we had together.

2 / Leaving Fort Bragg

9 Mar 03 – I received the call at 0630 to bring all my gear to the 0900 formation because we may be leaving later that day. After that formation, I spent the morning frantically packing last minute items. At noon I delivered two duffels, one rucksack and one carry-on bag for loading and then spent the afternoon sitting around waiting in the winter sun and making several last minute phone calls to family and friends. We loaded onto vans and buses at 1700 for the ride to Green Ramp at Pope AFB. I was finally reunited with Ana, Noah, Logan and Caroline at around 1900 hours.

They visited with me for about an hour and then left because the kids were rowdy and excited about all the activity, but they needed to get home and get ready for bed. The other reason for them to not wait around was that I didn't want my last memory to be one of getting frustrated with them because they were being kids. At 2345 hours we lined up for boarding of an ATA aircraft commissioned for our trip. We were wheels up sometime after midnight, and the reality hit me like a ton of bricks that we were really going.

10 Mar 03 – The first leg of the flight was around six hours, and we landed in Shannon, Ireland for fueling. The last leg was around seven hours and we arrived in Kuwait City around 2200 local time on the 10th. We signed into country and rode shielded buses to Camp Wolf less than two miles away. We received our initial briefing then were sent to an overcrowded tent for the rest of the night, sleeping on plywood floors. At this point, we only had our carry-on bags, which, in my case, didn't contain a toothbrush or any other personal hygiene items.

11 Mar 03 – Morning brought breakfast in a tent with hot meals, cereals, fruit and yogurt, and personal hygiene with a borrowed

disposable razor. The rest of the day was spent like cats – eating, sleeping – all the while being told, "Get ready, we're moving out in 15 minutes." In the afternoon, we moved again by buses to Camp Doha, which is the most established Army facility in Kuwait, having been here since the prior desert war. Camp Doha provided us cots in a large warehouse and reunited us with our bags and rucks. I enjoyed the shower facilities at 2300 hours and retired to the first full night's sleep in more than forty-eight hours that was not on an airplane or plywood floor.

12 Mar 03 – Breakfast in the main dining hall at Camp Doha was wonderful – cereal with skim milk, incredible fresh fruit, and decent coffee. I placed a collect call to Ana after breakfast at the ATT phone center. Rumor had it that we'd be there about four days with much time spent receiving our equipment and doing inventory. So far, the morning had been spent reading, napping, and now writing this. Afternoon was very much the same, and then at 1900 we received "the briefing" to describe our mission. In spite of expecting this news, it collectively took our breath away. Immediately we began to plan the execution of our mission. Soon thereafter, the storm hit. It was the infamous sand storm that we'd been expecting since the day before. It was as impressive as any weather phenomenon I have seen. The visibility was non-existent. The best place to be was indoors, but our warehouse quickly filled with nearly as much dust as outside. It covered everything, including us, and I went to sleep with the goggles and "neck-gator" in place on my face.

13 Mar 03 – The morning was hazy, as usual, and showed the effects of the previous night's sand storm. After breakfast I set about to cleaning my area and doing laundry. Later in the day the combination of a shower, clean clothes, and a nice, relaxed dinner at the dining facility left me feeling the best I had since leaving the states.

16 Mar 03 – It's Sunday here at Camp Doha and Bill D. and I went to Bible study and Protestant Worship here at the chapel. The service was well attended by members of the 28th CSH, and the sermon was good. The afternoon brought some more pretty useless meetings and more napping. The highlight of the evening was being

able to watch the NASCAR race from Darlington, live on the Armed Forces Network. It began at 2100 local and lasted until just after midnight. The finish was one of the most thrilling I'd ever seen. We plan to do the same next week if we are still here.

17 Mar 03 – At this stage, the days are all pretty much the same. We spend our waking hours finding things to fill the time. Some of the leaders want to make it more productive by having classes and training, while most of the doctors want the downtime to pursue pleasant endeavors like wandering in the Post Exchange (PX), going to the Red Cross room to watch the news, or going to the Multi-Media center to write and answer e-mails. Usually, we will leave for breakfast and just do not come back. President Bush is scheduled to address the nation tonight at 2000 EST, but it will be 0400 on 18 Mar for us. We expect him to deliver an ultimatum. We will get the details at breakfast via CNN or Fox News on the TVs in the dining facility (DFAC).

19 Mar 03 – Bill is beside me in the warehouse, and we are hanging out together. We eat, watch the news in the Red Cross room, cruise the PX, visit the multi-media center, and watch movies at Frosty's Oasis (where we watched the race). They had been showing real movies in the theater until today. All movies have been halted until further notice. Camp Doha is now less crowded as all the war fighters have moved into position near the border, getting ready to roll. Our hospital still has many logistical challenges to solve before we can follow. President Bush's deadline expires tonight at 0400 local time, which will actually be 20 Mar. We are all waiting expectantly.

20 Mar 03 – The war began in this time zone.

21 Mar 03 – I did not write yesterday because the past 24 hours has been filled with multiple "Scud Alerts" – nine as of right now since about 1230 yesterday. At first we were a little disoriented, but now they are becoming easier to deal with. An alert requires that we go to mission oriented protective posture (MOPP) level 4, which consists of gas mask, tops/bottom clothing, hood, gloves, and boots. The alert usually lasts 15–25 minutes and then the "All Clear" is given, and we can remove our masks. Because there have been so

many, we are now constantly in MOPP level 1, which is the outer garments over our normal uniforms. Needless to say, our body temperature is significantly higher. Fortunately, none of the scuds have threatened us, but we heard the Patriot anti-scud missiles that are located near us fire off during the second alert.

During the 1st three alerts, Bill and I went into bunkers that are outside our warehouse. That very first episode caused me to have a small panic attack of sorts, and I had to remove my mask for 1–2 minutes while it passed. Bill thinks it was caused by my position; sitting with my knees up against my chest in the crowded, low-ceilinged bunker. Regardless, for those brief moments, I was sure that my next breath was not coming unless that mask came off. Since then the alerts have been better tolerated, and most of the time we now just stay here in the warehouse.

The DFAC stopped serving meals as of breakfast this morning, and I have eaten little because the MRE's do not appeal to me at the present. I am sure that will change, as I get hungry. Plans now call for us to leave Camp Doha tomorrow and go to Camp Victory, which is a staging area for us to eventually join the large support convoy that will be rolling north into Iraq. Of course, all of this comes against the backdrop of the war having started "Operation Iraqi Freedom."

We have been watching coverage on Fox News at the Red Cross area. As of right now the effort is going well, and we are achieving key strategic objectives in western, southern, and southeastern Iraq. Wouldn't it be wonderful if the path to Baghdad were easy enough to allow us to see no action? I don't think any of the members of the 28th would mind at all. Bill and I have decided that we'd just as soon avoid any future deployment where people shoot at you. We have not really enjoyed the past 36 hours.

22 Mar 03 – According to our mission brief, the initial hospital will be 44 beds with an emphasis on critical-care. When we enter Iraq we will stop near Karballa to assist the 212th Mobile Army Surgical Hospital (MASH) in their efforts as necessary. Then our mission calls for us to proceed forward to a position on the western side of the Euphrates River near Baghdad and establish our hospital

there. The remainder of the CSH will remain in Kuwait but will soon send forward more supplies and personnel and expand us to a 96-bed facility. With this plan, we will be the most forward positioned CSH in Iraq.

Today we are leaving Camp Doha for Camp Victory. Advance parties have said that Camp Victory is not very crowded, has a meal tent, shower trailers, and plywood flooring in the tents. There is also decent electrical access in the sleep tents for our computers and rechargeable items. At present there is no phone or email access. My biggest drawback to going there is that there are no flushing toilets. There is no official word on how long we may be at Camp Victory, but speculation is a week or even longer, depending on the course of the war. As of this morning, the big "shock and awe" air campaign has still not been delivered. The rest of the strategic military targets are being taken decisively. Fox News was reporting that footage exists showing "panicked digging" the night of the initial bombing and suspicion that Saddam Hussein was loaded into an ambulance on a stretcher. Thankfully, so far there have been only 6 American casualties.

Bill left in the first wave this morning for Camp Victory and will secure us a good location in the sleep tents there. The PX and all the shops here are now closed. We have been blocked from e-mail as of 2 days ago, but phones are still on, and I talked to Ana yesterday. In spite of the situation I find myself in, I believe that God is good and is sustaining me every day in ways that are reassuring and tangible.

(Later in the day) Well, I thought Bill was leaving this morning, but they didn't leave until ~1430, so my group won't be going today to Camp Victory. This is another example of the kinds of things that keep happening to this CSH. I am still not convinced we will accomplish anything meaningful either during or after the war is over. We're still in our warehouse, but we packed up all our cots and turned them back in. We'll see what the night brings.

(Later still) We brought the cots back out and slept with our MOPP suits on. I didn't even need my sleeping bag. Since we didn't depart Camp Doha I was able to call home and speak to Ana and the kids, including Logan, who was preparing for his birthday party. He was already enjoying a gift from me, a package that Ana had mailed to him and told him it was from me. Talking to him lifted my spirits tremendously.

23 Mar 03 – Today is Logan's fifth birthday, and I can't help but be somewhat dejected that I am here spinning my wheels rather than there spending it with him. I promise myself that in the future I will minimize the amount of time that I am away from family. At 1100 we loaded 17 people into the back of our five-ton truck. Several of us were literally lying atop the bags stacked in the middle of the floor. We finally rolled out and made it to Camp Victory without incident in about 90 minutes.

The DFAC is very acceptable with two hot meals per day – breakfast and dinner. No eating in the tents, and showers are every 3rd day. It is incredibly dark here at night when the sun goes down. Lights are out at 2200.

24 Mar 03 – We were briefed today that the higher command is asking us to be ready to join the convoy and roll north as soon as possible. We still have several showstopper items missing that prevent us from doing that. However, the time is drawing nearer whether I like it or not. Yesterday I saw Tamara M., who was a classmate of mine in residency. She is here with the 21st CSH from Ft Hood, Texas. She told me that they were briefed for their mission, and it sounds almost identical to ours. However, they are waiting for their equipment to arrive and have been here almost a week. Our convoy is virtually complete and ready.

This afternoon we spent over an hour drilling for convoy procedures and learning how to defend our convoy if we are being attacked. Bill and I decided that we'd all be in very bad shape if they were relying upon us doctors or medical staff to provide defense. However, with the recent news of the capture of the convoy near An Nasiriyah, we are all listening very closely to what they are instructing us.

The war is not going as well as it was initially, and I suppose we should have expected that, but I am still a bit dejected. I am sad to think about the lives being lost, but I still believe our cause is justifiable. We just need to finish the deal and get it done. We are hearing nothing now about the Saddam Hussein storyline.

26 Mar 03 – Yesterday was one of the most unusual, yet pleasant days that we have spent since being out of the United States. The temperature was in the 60's, and it was windy and raining on and off for most of the daylight hours. The dusty sand became wet and packed, just like along the edge of the surf at the beach. The majority of mindless training was cancelled, and we mostly laid around in our tents reading, playing cards, and listening to the radio. Our relaxation was interrupted in the afternoon by another "Scud" alert, which, at Camp Victory, requires us to quickly don our Kevlar helmets and flack vests and run to the trenches or cement barriers. Since arriving here we have had four alerts by my count, bringing the total to some number that I cannot remember. To say they are becoming very annoying is an understatement.

Late yesterday we were briefed that the forward package of 44 beds would move out no earlier than 1200 today and no later than 72 hours after that. The remaining personnel and equipment to round out a 96-bed facility would leave 4–7 days later. Our destination is a position north of the Karballa Pass near the Euphrates River to the west of Baghdad. At present, we hear that forces of the 3rd Infantry Division (ID) are fighting in and around the Karballa Pass and trying to secure that advance. Most of us would feel much better knowing that the threat in the area had been eliminated before we leave on our convoy.

A forecasted sandstorm arrived last night at about 0030 hours and threatened our tent. We were able to reinforce the poles to keep the walls from falling, but the enlisted females were not so lucky. Their tent fell, and we worked about an hour retrieving their gear and getting them divided into the other tents. The winds didn't truly die down until about 1100 this morning. When we awoke, the temperature was colder than yesterday, and the visibility from the sand blowing around was less than 200 yards. This truly is a surreal place.

We were allowed a shower yesterday. It was the first one in several days and may be the last true shower for quite a while. The plans for the 44-bed package do not include showers and laundry. Our commander has reminded us that we may have to suck it up for a while. Isn't that what we've been doing for more than four weeks now?

28 Mar 03 – Today was a beautiful day here, sunny and without a cloud in the sky. The temperature was much warmer, and many people took advantage of the weather to do laundry.

Yesterday would have been my father's 77th birthday if he were still living. I thought about him quite a bit and wrote a long letter home to Ana and the kids. My father had served in the Pacific in World War II. I wondered how "his" war differed from mine. I wondered if I had become the man he had hoped I would be. And I wondered if he would be proud of me.

We still have not received any mail or packages from home, and that is a morale buster. We were briefed yesterday that the forward package should leave tomorrow morning. We will be in MOPP 1 when we depart here and will likely remain that way for the foreseeable future. If we do not leave tomorrow, it will be because the main supply route (MSR) is still not safe enough for support vehicles due to insurgents in the towns along the way.

I cut my hair again today, although this time it is really short. Earlier this week I had it cut down to 3/8" on top and 1/8" on the sides, faded in. Today, it all came off. In addition to it feeling much cooler and being low maintenance, I like the way it looks. I know Ana won't care for it, but she had allowed that it would probably be a desirable thing to do once I was here. I took some pictures looking at myself in the mirror, which should turn out fairly humorous. Aside from when I was born, I think this is the shortest it has ever been. Pretty much all the other physicians have done the same thing. Bill thinks he started a trend, but it doesn't count in his case since he was "hair challenged" to begin with.

Speaking of the other doctors, some of our "combat" specialists include one gastroenterologist, two cardiologists, two cardiothoracic surgeons, a liver transplant surgeon, two urologists, two obstetricians, three general surgeons, three orthopedists, a radiologist, a psychiatrist, and several anesthesiologists. In total, it is a fairly impressive group of brainpower that is patiently waiting to set up our hospital and begin to do our real jobs of patient care. Life will be so much better then.

3 / The Convoy into Iraq

30 Mar 03 – We actually left Camp Victory yesterday morning as planned at around 1130. After a surprisingly emotional farewell formation from the soldiers remaining behind, we proceeded north to the Iraqi border. After linking up with our Military Police escort, our convoy of 45 vehicles crossed into Iraq around 1730 on 29 Mar 03. The Iraqi border town we passed through was an extremely impoverished one. Many Iraqis lined the roadway for miles; some shook fists, but most gave us the thumbs up sign, especially the children.

We had been briefed that once in Iraq, we would travel approximately four hours until we reached Tallil, an airbase under coalition control. During the evening I was lying in the floorboard of our 5-ton truck, waiting for the convoy to stop. I dozed off to sleep, like many of the others, and was awakened at around 0100 when we stopped for bathroom breaks. Unfortunately, we loaded up again and continued driving, often without lights, until we reached our destination at around 0430. The trip was apparently prolonged because of vehicle breakdowns, flat tires, concealment issues, and misjudgment of speed and distances. The latter was the work of the commander. I think there is a joke in there somewhere about having a female in charge of the map and directions. I was extremely cold during the night because the friendly daytime breeze became evil as the sun went down and night fell.

We awoke in the morning not knowing when we would leave and began to explore the surroundings. We were beside an airfield that our USAF is using for flight operations. Nearby was a large wall over 20 feet high with a mural of Saddam Hussein painted on it. Some have left written messages on the wall. This experience is beginning to feel somewhat like a camping trip gone extremely awry.

It's currently mid-afternoon and we are waiting to receive more tires (to replace the ones gone flat), more fuel, and our next security element for the ride farther north. The 86th CSH from Fort Campbell, Kentucky, is located here. We are trying to borrow these items from them because this is supposed to be their final destination, and they are tasked with primarily treating the Enemy Prisoners of War (EPW's).

We have come, by my viewing of the map, one-third of the way to our final objective. The next phase calls for us to proceed to where the 212th MASH is set up. There is still no mail to boost the morale, and I don't know how it will find us when it starts to come. We certainly have been nomadic, and I really miss Ana, the kids, and the American way. However, I honestly felt a great sense of high adventure yesterday on that initial convoy into Iraq. We are tired and bored, but we are finally in "Indian country," and that has added another element to all that is happening.

31 Mar 03 – We spent the day yesterday at Tallil waiting for our security escort to arrive to take us farther north. It never came, and by late in the day we had broken out our cots and were set to sleep under the stars of Iraq. As dusk approached we had a prayer and praise service standing around the big mural of Saddam. I became pretty emotional during the prayer service, and I had chill bumps throughout as believers stood there in Iraq praising God beside that big mural.

The next day we left Tallil around 1300 hours and drove along an alternate supply route (ASR) out to a main supply route (MSR) that took us south for about an hour to a Convoy Support Center where we were to meet our escorts. We waited for what seemed like an eternity in that dusty spot and then left, again without any additional escort or security measures. The three-lane MSR we came down on was deemed too insecure, so we left around 1700 on a miserable ASR headed in a generally northwest direction. The road was a mixture of sand and broken pavement, which left us all covered in dust and beaten about.

Along the way we encountered many Iraqi families who were living a nomadic lifestyle out in the desert, herding their sheep and goats. Aside from the old buses and trucks that we occasionally saw, I felt like we could have been driving around in biblical times. As darkness fell we could see scattered lights on occasion, but mostly it was very dark. We only had one tire blow out in the cooler temperatures. During one rest stop, our convoy reportedly received indirect fire off to our right front. Several of us saw flashes, but I never heard the explosions.

01 Apr 03 – After traveling more than 12 hours, we arrived at dawn at Objective Bushmaster where the 212th MASH is located. We parked and offered our services to them. They respectfully declined most of our assistance. They were treating mostly EPW's and Iraqi civilians. The US soldiers were rapidly evacuated more rearward after being stabilized. Our plan was to stay three or four days, depending on how the forward war effort progressed. The formal attack on the Karballa Gap and the push toward Baghdad began tonight. As night fell we heard several track vehicles rolling by, and the sights and sounds of artillery were also close by.

We remain in MOPP 1 and went to MOPP 4 several times during the day because of false positive alerts on the chemical sensors posted around the perimeter of the compound. It turns out that several of these sensors are located downwind from the latrines and are reacting to the strong detergents being used to aid in decomposition. Once this was recognized, the sensors were moved and the number of alerts dropped rapidly.

In mid-morning I was laying on my cot gazing upward just in time to see an explosion directly over our heads. It was a missile that came from a Patriot battery located nearby and impacted on something in the air. Of course, this prompted another MOPP 4 alert, but in this case, few seemed to mind. Eventually we were given the "all clear" and resumed our task of doing nothing. Later in the day we were tasked with erecting tents and digging latrines, all in MOPP 1. It looks like we might stay longer than we thought.

02 Apr 03 – We awoke this morning to a MOPP 4 alert. I read my devotional and said prayers until the "all clear" came. The weather

is getting hotter during the days, and we are still strictly in MOPP 1, even though most other units we see around us are not. This place is one of the most miserable places I could imagine. The sand here is very fine, and it blows everywhere, even when you are just walking and trying to avoid kicking it up.

03 Apr thru 05 Apr 03 – These three days were very repetitive in the events that took place. I awoke each morning and wondered what I could do until dusk and the chance to sleep and be cool again. The days were miserably hot and dusty. We finally instituted a siesta policy during the hours of 1000–1400 hours where no work was to take place. I am down to eating a light breakfast and lunch of granola bars or crackers and then having an MRE for dinner.

I feel like a real infantry soldier because I am pooping in a hole in the ground in the desert. I can't bring myself to use the slit trenches near camp at this point; I prefer the solitude of the desert. The monotony of each day is broken by stupid formations to put out more non-information. The Army really stinks. The only redeeming thing about the 1700 formation is that it gives us a chance to have our daily prayer service afterwards. I continue to be thankful for our chaplain, Keith C., because God is surely working through him to sustain me and bring me closer in my daily walk. It's really sort of a shame that I had to come to Iraq to instill enough discipline in me to have a daily devotional and prayer time. It makes me think that God has many purposes for me being here, and making me a better Christian may be the primary one.

On the afternoon of our last day at Objective Bushmaster, I took one of our soldiers over to the 212th MASH to receive treatment for passing out. I had been treating him for hypertension, and I really feel like his symptoms were from excess medications and dehydration. While he was receiving fluids I had the opportunity to explore their operation and see some casualties for the first time. Most of them were Iraqis, both civilian and EPW's. Fortunately, the children I saw were minimally injured. I was surprised to find myself almost apprehensive about finally seeing the Iraqis up close. I'm not sure what I was expecting, but I found that they were just humans in need because of the circumstances.

There were very few US soldiers because their air-evacuation system was working well, and they were moving people out fairly rapidly. The capacity of that MASH is about 35–40 beds, but the big difference from us is that they can be fully mobile within 12–24 hours. I took advantage of it being cool, and I allowed myself to feel like a physician again for a little while. I even got to read an electrocardiogram (EKG).

That evening we observed communion in the desert because we were preparing to make the final push to our destination. It was a moving experience because the war was literally going on around us, and Keith reminded us for perspective that we were not too far from the ruins of Babylon.

4 / Establishing 28CSH-Dogwood

07 Apr 03 – We arrived at Objective Dogwood in the early morning hours after another grueling convoy spanning 13 hours, and again, without any adequate security protection. This segment of the trip brought us up through the Karballa Gap, which was fairly unimpressive, and we didn't feel any real threat. We passed through a deserted Iraqi military compound that was interesting to see, even in the darkness.

Dogwood is located in the desert approximately 15 miles southwest of Baghdad. While the staking team laid out the hospital boundaries, the rest of us cleared the land of the scrub brush and began erecting our sleep tents. We worked until dusk and enjoyed another MRE for dinner. All the entrées taste the same, regardless of what the bag says. The Lord has surely sustained and placed a hedge of protection around us to this point, and it is time to get down to the business of being a hospital.

09 Apr 03 – We spent yesterday working our behinds off to get our hospital constructed. We still have no mail and have received thanks only from Keith for our hard work. Our sleep tents are filled with the most dust of any place we have lived so far. The commander promised us that our conditions would grow progressively more austere, and she is determined to live up to her promise. Our morale is biphasic; our living conditions stink, but our hospital is now almost complete.

At 1730 we accepted our first patient from an air-evacuation in Baghdad. He was a soldier from the 3rd ID who had been injured by a rocket-propelled grenade (RPG) and sustained a scratch on his eyeball and a very small skin abrasion on his lower abdomen from a piece of shrapnel. He was easily stabilized, treated, and evacuated by ground to a nearby unit who could provide him holding capacity overnight. He told us that the battle in Baghdad was very one-sided; their infantry against our tanks. He said there were many Iraqi people openly celebrating our presence in the streets.

10 Apr 03 – Last night we smoked a cigar in celebration of "arriving." This morning I continued the celebration by doing a baby wipe shower and changing my uniform. I also had the good fortunes of having hot water for coffee this morning. We were given Canadian MRE's today for variety. With coffee mugs in hand and fresh clothes on, Bill and I headed to work in the hospital. Bill joked that all we needed were briefcases to carry. Right now, the hospital is the desirable place to be because that is where the air-conditioning is on.

Let the official medical command historical record reflect that at 1305 hours MAJ Dixon and MAJ (P) Hodges admitted the first three patients to the 28th CSH. They were all EPW's transferred from the nearby Area Support Medical Company. The injuries consisted of a 31-year-old with a gunshot wound (GSW) to the chest, a 22-year-old with a GSW to his face resulting in a jaw fracture and GSW to the legs resulting in a leg fracture, and a 39-year-old with a GSW thru his abdomen and wrist.

Later there were two other admissions, both American, and both with orthopedic injuries who were primarily managed by the orthopedists. Early in the evening we evacuated Iraqi patient number 1 and 2. Patient number 3 was held to resolve his respiratory status and to explore his wrist injury operatively. There were several more false alarms of admissions, but none came. I spent the first night in the ICU "on call," which means I slept on one of the beds in the corner of the unit that wasn't being used. Bill and I have decided to both work during daylight hours and take every other night call. Our area of responsibility, at present, is two ICU's and one ward.

We have a Kuwaiti interpreter who is marginally effective in his role. His command of English is not the best; I can only hope that his Arabic is better. He is short and rotund and fancies himself as quite the worldly ladies' man. It is quite humorous to watch him hit on all the females. They, of course, are repulsed by his invasion of their personal space and his ever-present aroma. He doesn't do a very good job of hiding his disdain for all Iraqis.

13 Apr 03 – The past two days have proven the old phrase in a different nation: "If you build it, they will come." Fortunately for our soldiers, their visits have been rare. Unfortunately for the Iraqis, they have visited often, and many are remaining until we can move them farther south or out to Iraqi hospitals. On a happier note, Bill's son John Henry arrived on 11 Apr 03 weighing 5 pounds, 9 ounces and is doing well. Bill was able to talk to Shannon before and after delivery, and she also is doing well. Bill and I enjoyed two Cohiba cigars last night, compliments of Steve W. Pictures were taken and will be sent along with e-mail messages. I received my first set of mail two nights ago.

Today is Palm Sunday, and we had an extremely good worship service. We were hot and dusty in an unused tent, but we made the best of it. The worship services here are excellent, and that has been the best surprise about this whole deployment. We have praise singing, prayer time, and wonderful, Scripture-based messages from our chaplain, Keith.

15 Apr 03 – It is tax day back home, but I think this hospital paid its taxes yesterday. We experienced our first American fatalities yesterday afternoon over the course of a couple of hours. The first incident involved a young soldier who was brought into the Emergency Medical Treatment (EMT) section basically dead on arrival with a good portion of his face missing. One of our cardiothoracic surgeons, Tom, cracked his chest and did open cardiac massage with no results. Shortly thereafter, a chopper brought in four more soldiers who had been victims of an explosion in a Humvee. The driver and his friend, standing outside the vehicle, suffered the brunt of the explosion and did not survive. The passengers in the front and rear seats sustained concussions and minor shrapnel injuries.

The mood throughout the CSH noticeably changed. My own personal opinion of the Iraqi patients changed somewhat as well. I began to be apathetic toward continuing to give them optimal care. I could also easily see the same attitude in the faces of everyone else around me. For days we have struggled with being able to make distinctions between the civilians and enemy prisoners of war (EPW's). Surprisingly, it is often difficult to tell the difference between good guy and bad guy, and our military intelligence and civil affairs folks aren't necessarily able to help, either. I think we are drifting toward a policy where all Iraqis may need to be restrained if they are undergoing treatment here. The complications then arise about what to do with the parents of the children we are treating — should we be restraining them also?

Over the past several days I have been talking with an injured Iraqi man who is a 39-year-old civil engineer and speaks fairly fluent English. He lives in Baghdad and told me that he was driving from his home in the city to a shopping area to buy supplies for his family when he pulled into an alley to park. Upon exiting his car, American tanks suddenly came by and engaged a target near him, trapping him in the crossfire of the battle. His left shoulder muscle was blown off, and his back and chest were literally peppered with shrapnel. He also had soft tissue damage to his nose, face, right forearm and left leg. He was initially treated by a Forward Surgical Team (FST) and then placed in their medical holding company. He was transferred to us after developing a fever one day later. Our surgeons explored and cleaned his wounds again and then left me to diagnose and manage his pneumonia.

Over the course of the day we discussed several neutral topics, such as his command of English and his family. He claims that he learned English from American monks who lived in Baghdad when he was in secondary school. The monks left Iraq but left their books behind. Eventually I felt the need to apologize to him for us causing injuries to the innocent people of Iraq. He asked me if I thought our President was purely interested in getting rid of Saddam in order to give him his freedom. I told him I was not naïve enough to think that was the only reason and that economics was surely a factor. However, I told him that his freedom was the primary reason *we* were here, that and to preserve the freedom that our families felt back home. In the end I felt the conversation to have been successful in making my points to him.

Another 60 members of the hospital arrived last night to augment our staff. And they brought mail — lots and lots of mail. I alone received seven packages and numerous letters, some from friends of our friends that I don't even know. It was awesome to get a connection to home and family again and to read about how much support we are really getting back home. For the past 2+ weeks, we have been in a relative news vacuum. We had no idea that the folks at home were so behind us. I have more than enough snacks to last for a while. If we could get our sleep tents livable and the latrine situation upgraded, life would be much more tolerable. Right now, those two areas of our lives are almost unbearable.

18 Apr 03 — I have been busying myself with establishing somewhat of a routine, if that is possible here. My day starts early, usually soon after the sunrise, which is around 0600. We have rounds at 0700 as a medical staff, and then I have been recently going to another meeting with the commander, which is somewhat of a departmental chief's meeting. After the meetings, Bill and I divide the work as needed and go about our role of being hospitalists. We don't know each patient well, but we are trying to keep our fingers on the pulse of care (pun intentional) and assist the surgeons in their management without becoming their interns. So far, the working relationships are extremely good.

The recently arrived staff members are still putting up tents, beautifying the hospital compound, and generally paying their elusive "dues" for not having endured the initial convoy up here. Chris B. is a family physician and Dave H. is another internist. They are both anxious to begin work, and Bill and I are ready to have their help. We are tired of every other night call and look forward to establishing a nice, four person hospital practice with one-in-four call. Our workload and schedule will be much more normal then.

I haven't been able to read anything for pleasure since we opened for business ten days ago. The mail is coming daily now, and I have continued to get great packages. I am truly blessed by the efforts of my friends and families. Some of the other people are beginning to get jealous of my packages. One soldier joked that he thought I was getting mail about every four hours. I am sharing as much as I can and keeping only the really desirable things for myself. I certainly don't need any more toilet paper for now. They actually have a decent supply here; the latrines just leave much to be desired. I was beginning to enjoy doing my business in the desert, but the urban sprawl of the growing camp has pretty much surrounded us now.

The laundry and bath personnel started personal laundry services yesterday. We were allowed to turn in 15 items and should get them back in 48–72 hours. We'll see how that goes. Today and tomorrow are the scheduled shower days for the week for us, but I have found that if I go late at night, there is usually no problem getting one because I made friends with the sergeant who controls shower access. It's amazing how much you can make happen just by being friendly and not overly greedy. We still don't have reliable Internet access, and no one is able to reasonably explain why. I am also very confused by the phone call situation and our lack of access.

It is Good Friday, and we are planning a Bible study tonight with the chaplain. I confess that I have been too busy to reflect much on Passion Week. Two to three days ago we started to get very busy with many admissions and few transfers out. We are working very hard to establish an ongoing relationship with one or more of the local hospitals to transfer the numerous Iraqi civilians there. Our census has risen as high as 34 patients early yesterday out of a total of 42 beds. American soldiers make up less than one third. Their evacuation is much easier, sometimes happening later the same day.

I cared for three boys yesterday, unrelated and aged 5, 8, and 16, respectively. Shrapnel, mostly in the legs, had injured them all, but the five-year-old also had an abdominal injury. Fortunately, in the OR they found it was not penetrating, and they merely cleaned and dressed it. I was worried about how I would handle caring for patients who reminded me of Noah, Logan, or Caroline. All three of these boys reminded me of my children, but they were much more malnourished. It broke my heart inwardly, but I quietly prayed to God to strengthen my resolve and allow me to provide their care. The language barrier, both with the children and their parents, frustrates me. The fathers of the two younger boys were with them and both appropriately concerned and scared. Through the interpreters, I assured them that the wounds would heal fine. I have yet to meet an Iraqi parent, child, or even most EPW's who are not genuinely grateful for our help. It is gratifying yet bizarre in some ways because the hostilities have not fully ended, and it's easy to lose sight of what is going on outside these walls.

Last night was a beautiful night here, cool with a full moon crossing the sky. In the moonlight, the desert landscape here looks just like a big snow has fallen. The dust covering the tents and generators just adds to that illusion. I sat outside for a while looking at the moon and staring at the skies, listening to a Nora Jones CD my friends sent me. I had never heard it before, but it seemed to be the perfect choice of music for the evening. It was one of those experiences I have had in my life where the music was the perfect accompaniment to the surroundings and situation. I came inside the tent and easily fell into a restful sleep.

19 Apr 03 – Yesterday two Iraqi girls, aged 8 and 9, presented at the ER in need of scheduled blood transfusions. The only word their father knew was thalassemia. I called the pediatrician, Rick B., who is nearby at the 549th ASMC, and he came over to aid me in managing these girls. He concluded that based on their history of monthly transfusions, they most likely had a disease called beta-thalassemia major, which he had never seen. Their red blood cell counts were high, they had enormous livers and spleens on exam, and their facial appearance was somewhat funny looking. They were also very pale, almost yellow in color, and lacked any significant color in their skin creases. We were able to transfuse each of them one unit of blood without complications. A very friendly and concerned Engineer Corps captain, who is responsible for the sector they live in, escorted them back home. I had my picture taken with the family before they left. I am not sure if we'll see them again or not. The reason they came was that they'd been unable to get blood since the war started.

Last night we held Bible study and took communion to observe Good Friday. My spiritual needs continue to be met, and I can only give God the praise and glory for leading me where I need to be, even if it took me coming to Iraq to get there. My favorite song while here has become "I Can Only Imagine" by Mercy Me, partly because of the awesome message and partly because I think Ana is very fond of it as well. It connects me with her spiritually every time I listen to it. I am almost at the point that I can listen to it now without crying.

As I had mentioned earlier, I now attend a daily meeting with the commander that includes all the departmental chiefs, of which I am one. The meeting was fairly typical this morning until she dropped the bombshell that we had been given warning orders to begin to prepare to jump the original 32-bed package farther forward, more north of Baghdad. She stated that the feeling amongst the combat support services was that the best use of medical assets was to have several small, mobile facilities spread all around. I thought the four clinicians present at the meeting showed remarkable restraint initially. Then we launched our all out frontal assault against her and what we thought was a very stupid idea. We went on to explain that the lessons we had learned from just being set up here argued very strongly against the concept of further diluting the medical capabilities. It is clear that we had not expected the patients here to be this sick, require this much OR time, and stay this long in our facility.

Dave H. and Chris B. are ready to begin work and will do the next two nights of call, giving Bill and me some needed rest. It will be the beginning of our four-person call schedule that will give us all a day off every fourth one.

20 Apr 03 – It is Easter Sunday, and today's journal entry will double as an open letter to everyone back home. I was able to get a shower last night, and it was amazing. It's incredible how good hot water can feel, even if it only comes once a week and lasts for four minutes. Many of the soldiers and patients we treat do not even have that small luxury.

Two days ago the dining hall ran out of coffee. They quickly learned that contrary to the thoughts about blood, supplies, etc., hospitals really run on coffee. Fortunately, that problem is now rectified, and the situation has returned to normal. The MRE's have instant coffee packets in them, but it is not the same.

My spiritual growth through the worship services and prayer groups has been the most pleasant and meaningful surprise for me on this whole deployment. Our chaplain, Keith C., is a Southern Baptist minister by training, and he truly believes in exhorting us to put feet to our faith. His message today about living our lives with regard to a risen Lord was very pertinent to our evolving mission here, that of caring for the Iraqi civilians and enemy prisoners of war (EPW's).

It is difficult at times to remain constantly compassionate toward the non-Americans here when the choppers off-load soldiers who have been injured. Sometimes our wards are housing a mixture of patients. I can only imagine what would run through my mind if I were a wounded American soldier lying in a bed thirty feet away from an Iraqi EPW. However, I was convicted by the message today that we have a tremendous ministry opportunity here if we can conduct ourselves in a manner that uplifts Jesus by our compassion.

Yesterday was very hectic, with multiple admissions and 11 surgeries needing to be performed. Several soldiers were injured, and a young Iraqi girl died after she was handed an explosive device and told to carry it to them.

Another group of two women and a four-year-old girl were transferred from a local hospital. They had all been burned severely, and their injuries were not fresh. One of the women died shortly after arriving. The little girl is burned over a large percentage of her body and has only a 20–30% chance of surviving.

The Iraqi citizens and EPW's are a problem, and we end up keeping them for longer than was projected. We are beginning to face the same problems as any hospital back home when people stay for long periods of time. We are hampered by limited supplies, and our laboratory capabilities are not at their fullest. All of this combines to frustrate the medical staff that has the knowledge and skill to be able to do more, but currently lacks the tools.

Fragment injuries to the extremities are the most common injury for the American soldiers because their gear protects their torsos and heads. The EPW's have little protective gear and tend to be much more severely injured than we had anticipated.

As expected, it is dealing with the younger patients that gives me and all the other staff the most difficulty. I have observed that the look of concern on a parent's face spans all nationalities and faiths. My heart goes out to these children and their parents when they are here.

Redeployment, or coming home, was mentioned for the first time the other day, and the rough time frame was mentioned as being October/November. That is a little longer than I had hoped, but that is a long time away, and many things can happen. As I have for most of this deployment, I remain focused on today and maybe tomorrow. The rest will take care of itself.

I miss my family, my friends, and my country in the worst kind of way, but I am proud to be here for the ideals that we all believe in and for the freedom we all enjoy. It is a very sweet freedom indeed. I hope this letter finds all of you well, and I truly feel your prayers as your vigilance surrounds us all with God's protection. Please keep it up; we couldn't make it without you.

Sincerely,
Mike

22 Apr 03 – Today we learned about an article from the NY Times Internet site that dealt with the 28th CSH. I think it was dated yesterday. Many people from the 21st CSH and other units (212th MASH, Forward Support Battalions of the 82nd, etc.) have been stopping by to see our setup and learn from our experiences. We have opened our doors wide and have warmly welcomed everyone in.

The four-year-old girl is much more ill. Her burns are primarily of her head, face, hands, and feet. Her parents were both killed in the initial explosion. She has generated tremendous interest here in the hospital, with one of the nurses actually trying to adopt her and get her back to the US for definitive care. He has three other children and feels motivated to provide her a home also. Our hearts are all breaking for her. Naturally, his desire to adopt has really stirred the pot at much higher levels and rumor has it going all the way up to Donald Rumsfeld. She was re-intubated yesterday for respiratory distress, and she appears to be consumed with an infection in her blood and is requiring aggressive fluids and drugs to raise her blood pressure. I use these drugs routinely in my adult patients, but this is new territory in someone so small.

We have yet to receive our first shipment of pediatric supplies, things which we "emergency ordered" several days ago. The Army logistic supply system doesn't work, period. We learned from the commander this morning that the NSN (national stock number) that we have been scurrying around to find for all these supplies is different depending on whether you are ordering from US or Europe. As far as I'm concerned, that is classic for how broken the Army is.

I was able to talk to Ana and the kids yesterday by using the Army phone and being connected to Ramstein Germany, then Dover AFB, then to an ATT calling card line. Even with the bad connection, static, and voice delays, it was divine to hear their voices. I received the letters yesterday dated 15 and 16 Mar, which are probably some of the first ones mailed from home. The mail system is not ideal at present, but at least is trickling in now.

24 Apr 03 – We assisted three enlisted soldiers with the construction of our floor in the sleep tents today. Really, we provided most of the labor, seeing as how there were only three of them, and the only tools they had were three hammers and one saw. Our orthopedists were the most helpful, go figure, and had tape measures, hammers, nails, and saws. Working together, we finished in about 2–3 hours. Then we moved the stuff back in and put the sandbags back in place on the outside. The dining tent now has tables and chairs for us to sit at. Wow, what a difference that makes. The improvements are slowly coming, but they are coming each day.

Today, Dr. Bob Arnott of MSNBC/CNBC came to the hospital with a film crew and told the story of the four-year-old girl. I was not around, but Bill and some of the other staff were interviewed. A Saudi Arabian physician who is a plastic surgeon familiar with burn injuries accompanied Dr. Arnott. Apparently the Saudis now plan on taking her to their hospital along with the lady who was burned and another three-year-old boy who was admitted today with 20–30% burns.

The neurosurgery team is now up here with us and will have

their equipment arriving soon so that they can do surgery. Their team also includes a neurologist.

We acquired an area off the storage room, and it is becoming a popular place for people to hang out because we have our own air-conditioning. We have named it "The Flea Bag," and even the surgeons are beginning to hang out here, especially when we watch movies. Our medical staff is as fine a group of physicians as I have ever known or worked with. Almost to a person, they all are dedicated and hard working. For the most part, they are easy-going, and the personalities seem to complement instead of clash. Needless to say, it has made the patient care aspect of this deployment most enjoyable.

25 Apr 03 – The big news this morning was a US soldier who came to us after having committed suicide by placing his weapon in his mouth and pulling the trigger. There was no treatment to render. Our four-year-old burn girl is improving and has been weaned off the pressure drugs. She and the older woman were debrided in the OR yesterday and seemed to tolerate it well. No further word on whether they will transfer today or not.

27 Apr 03 – Recently I had been wishing that I would get the opportunity to leave the 10 acre compound that makes up the 28th CSH. On Saturday the 26th, I got the opportunity that I was hoping for. Our patient administration division informed us that the 30th Medical Brigade Commander, who is our higher headquarters, had arranged for physicians in Saudi Arabia to accept our high profile, four-year-old burn patient. He had also arranged for them to accept the other burn patient, who was a female teacher in her late twenties. The plan called for us to take them by ground ambulance to Baghdad International Airport (BIAP). We were to travel by ground ambulance because the strong shamal winds were still grounding our helicopter assets. I can testify that the shamal was still very much a factor because the day and night of the 25th had been spent worrying when one or all of our tents were going to go down. The night of the 25th was the worst night we had spent since our convoy up here because the winds were of unbelievable strength, and the temperature would not drop. I spent the night sleeping on top

of my sleeping bag and awoke to find myself literally covered in layers of dust. It took countless baby wipes to achieve any sense of normalcy.

We loaded our patients into two separate ambulances with Dave H. and a nursing aide riding with the lady, and myself, an ICU nurse, and a respiratory therapist riding with the girl. After finally leaving our perimeter and traveling a ways, we were stuck for probably one hour in real-life Baghdad rush hour traffic on the three-lane freeway running into town. The reason for the traffic on a Saturday morning is that Thursday and Friday are their weekend. In total, a 15 mile trip ending up taking us over four hours and caused our IV pump and cardiac monitor to exhaust their battery supply. The only thing still working was the ventilator and a small, battery-powered oxygen monitor on the girl's toe. Those of you who know my shortcoming in regards to patience can imagine and laugh to yourself about what kind of mood I was in when we arrived.

At the airport medical holding facility, our Air Force friends were wonderful hosts while we settled in to wait for the arrival of the Saudi plane. Both patients had been extremely stable during transit and remained so while we waited. The estimated arrival time came and went by several hours, and we were finally informed at around 1800 by someone from the 30th Medical Brigade that the Saudis had been prevented from flying by weather in Riyadh and had rescheduled for the same time the next day. By now our patients were still stable but not as perky as when we arrived, mostly because the heat was strong, the flies were annoying, and they were both due for medications and dressing changes. In addition, the little girl had begun to drop her blood pressure slightly and was requiring more fluids.

Taking all this into account, I decided to try to get us all back to the CSH. After several calls back to the CSH for guidance and with night rapidly approaching, we were able to contact an air-evacuation element there at the airport that agreed, after no small amount of coaxing, to fly us home. They were from Ft Hood, Texas, and provided wonderful service to us. As best as I can recall, that was the second flight in a helicopter I have ever taken. It was a Blackhawk aircraft and in two words – it rocked! I don't see aviation medicine or flight surgery in my near future, but it was a thoroughly enjoyable experience. The patients also tolerated the flight well, and we arrived safely back at the CSH around 2100.

While we were away yesterday, I understand that the EMT section evaluated and treated a canine patient who belonged to the MP's. I don't know the specific diagnosis, but I understand the treatment was successful.

While preparing our four-year-old patient for repeat transport back to the airport this morning, she experienced a series of clinical events that caused us to cancel her transfer and work very hard throughout the day to stabilize her deteriorating condition. Our best clinical hunch is that she experienced a blood clot that traveled from her leg to her lungs, causing a serious problem with her oxygenation capability and her blood pressure regulation. We started anti-coagulation medicine to prevent any further clots from forming and struggled with very powerful chemicals to raise her blood pressure. Given the acuity of our other patients and the inadequacies of our supply system, we have run out of most of the pressure support medicine and today were relying on epinephrine (pure adrenaline) to maintain her pressure and even then, not succeeding at times.

28 Apr 03 – In spite of the best care that we could provide given our circumstances, our four-year-old girl died this morning at 0646. While we will never know for certain the cause of death, I am convinced that her death was related to the blood clot in her lung that was associated with having an adult size catheter in her leg vein. At the request of COL P., I am filing a formal incident report to document the potential harm we may have caused by not having the appropriate pediatric equipment and supplies. I am heartbroken along with the nursing staff and the other physicians who participated in her care. Intellectually I know that her suffering is complete and that she'll never be forced to face life in an Arab culture as a scarred female, but in the end, she began to remind me too much of my own daughter. We have all shed our tears and have tried to move on today because we have more patients who need our atten-

tion. The acuity of the Iraqi patients is so unbelievably high, and we cannot seem to get a moment to catch our breath.

29 Apr 03 – Today in the morning staff meeting with the commander, I asked her if it was possible to have a pediatrician assigned to us. We are getting better at some of the management, but none of us feel competent to continue managing all these assorted pediatric patients if the acuity is going to continue to be so high. With the evacuation of Iraqis becoming more problematic, we have raised the issue of what our capacity for care is going to be and what mechanism will we employ to limit admissions.

The nurses currently here have been working 12-hour shifts since we arrived, without any days off. They are worn out and in great need of time off. When I mentioned this to the commander this morning in the staff meeting, she said I needed to be careful with my wording because, "there are no days off in war time." I quickly rephrased and said they needed down time.

Even though conditions here are improving on a daily basis, I cannot begin to explain some of the living conditions. The latrine situation is the most consistently disgusting thing I have ever had to face. They continue to be constructed like old-fashioned outhouses with big steel buckets underneath the seat that must be pulled out and burned. If you are lucky, that will happen on a daily basis. The seat top is wood with holes cut into it. Another major drawback is that the latrines contain anywhere from 5–6 seats in a row, which causes me some real problems as I tend to really want privacy in situations involving personal business. The most disgusting thing to have happened to me lately was when I had to do business in the midst of the recent shamal. The latrines have four walls but no cover. I found myself sitting there with winds swirling sand in my eyes like in the movie "Twister" and having to literally grab pieces of toilet paper out of the air to use them. I joked later that there should be some award given us for combat pooping in these circumstances. I will definitely have a different standard for cleanliness when I return to US toilets.

5 / Sustainment Phase

01 May 03 – We received a "high value detainee" (HVD) yesterday, and the transferring physician said he wanted me to evaluate his cardiac status because he was having intermittent chest pain and had a cardiac history. He arrived early in the evening with his two MP escorts in tow. As with many prior wars, decks of playing cards have been printed with the faces of the 52 most-wanted people in the Iraqi regime. When I asked if he was on the cards, one of the MP's replied, "I can't say, sir, but if you use your imagination you can probably figure it out." We are now scrambling around to find a deck of those cards to compare his face to them. In terms of his cardiac status, I learned that he suffered from hypertension and a heart arrhythmia, but I determined that his chest pain was likely due to him being out of his medicines.

I evaluated him with labs, did an echocardiogram, and arranged to have him transferred back to the facility. His demeanor was very pleasant, and he, like almost all the other Iraqis, seemed genuinely appreciative for the care received. I know I am naïve about the whole war issue because I have yet to have truly hard feelings toward the patients I have treated. The practical side of me knows that they have all probably done some horrendous things in their lives; however, there is no evidence of that when they come within our walls. Not all the patients are happy, but I think they all realize they are receiving competent and compassionate care here.

The big news briefed yesterday was that the USS Comfort was looking to off-load its patients and sail home. We don't have a good report as of yet on how many patients that would mean. We did receive news that they were especially interested in transferring their burn patients here, even though we have spent the past two weeks making deals to get our own burn patients out of this relatively dirty environment. We added a plastic surgeon to our staff from the 47th CSH, but the conditions for skin grafting here is far less than ideal, even by wartime standards. The one fact we know for certain is that burn patients who have greater than 30% body surface area burns are an enormous drain on the personnel and supply system. As I have said before, the supply system has yet to demonstrate that it is capable of sustaining us, even as we stand now.

Most of us are continuing to take doxycycline each day to prevent malaria, although we haven't seen any mosquitoes. The biggest pest challenge we have is from scorpions in our sleeping tents. Along with the scorpions have come the big stories about the size of the "man-eating" critters that have been seen. So far, I have not had any untoward encounters. I still don't spend too much time in the tent, even with the flooring and lights, because the dust issue is so overwhelming.

02 May 03 – I spent the day today hanging around the tent, or "hooch," as almost everyone is defaulting to call our living areas. I'm not really sure what the derivation of that term is, but it is quite economical in its conveyance of information. My intent was to organize the boxes I had scattered around from the care packages received so far. With that mission accomplished, I then moved on to do some laundry. Unfortunately, the wind really kicked up at about that same time. I persisted and washed out one uniform and a pair of PT shorts. The rest of the items can wait and be washed by the laundry and bath folks. After washing, if you can really call it that, I hung things out to dry on the clotheslines, which are strung on both sides of our tent. The clothes dry quickly, which is good because it reduces the free sand coating that comes with anything hanging outside.

Today has been a more difficult day for my attitude and spirit. Yesterday was the National Day of Prayer in the US, and we held a special prayer service last evening after dinner. My attitude has sagged as I realize how much I dislike this place because of all the dust and the constant challenge to keep things clean. As I have mentioned before, I am somewhat of a clean freak, and the conditions here are beginning to stretch my limits of tolerance. I am disappointed because I hoped the dust wouldn't be as bad with the plywood floors installed. The problem is these winds just drive it around and it gets into the tents through every crack and small opening. Any item I touch, such as my sleeping bag, rucksack, duffle bag, or any of the boxes, gives off a dust cloud into the air, which then settles back onto everything else again. Bottom line is that I am having a bad day, and it's because of our environment. I have found that my mood is much better when I am in the hospital, but I can't stay there the whole time.

My HVD patient was finally able to transport today back to the detention facility. Transportation safety issues kept him from going yesterday. By reviewing the pictures on the cards, I feel that he was the eight of diamonds card, which listed him as a deputy minister of finance. That ranks him as number 28 on the list of most wanted.

03 May 03 – Last night was beautiful with cool temperatures, a cloudless sky, and no wind whatsoever. Aside from recurrent dreams of scorpions crawling on me – which never happened – it was just the kind of night I needed to improve my outlook. There was no staff meeting this morning because the commander, the DCCS, and the S3 have flown north to Tikrit for a medical mission briefing.

Osana is a six-year-old Iraqi boy brought by his parents to the ER because of a three-month history of nausea, vomiting, diarrhea, and overall malnutrition. His initial blood sugar was 503. By history he felt well, had no abdominal pain, and a quite voracious appetite, eating all sorts of MRE items in the ER.

By exam he was thin with a slightly protuberant abdomen. The thinness was most apparent in his extremities. His hair was fine and thin, and there were small cracks at the corners of his mouth. The remainder of his exam was unremarkable. (I have pictures) Dave H. felt that there was a significant malabsorption problem present that was causing an insulin resistance syndrome. The problem in management with him came in being able to restrict him from eating too much of the junk food that is omnipresent from the care packages. The interesting point of the presentation is that today we were able to identify the parasite giardia in his stool specimen. Giardiasis is a fairly common infection in the US among hikers and campers, who get it by drinking infected water along ridges and mountain trails. The acute phase is usually manifest by really impressive diarrhea (termed explosive in some sources) and is easily treated. We don't normally see the chronic form, which can be severe and cause some of the manifestations we are seeing here. We feel that it is contributing significantly in this little boy and will treat it accordingly and see what happens.

On a personal side, he is a very pleasant little boy with a sweet spirit. He has already been a pleasure for the staff to work with. I think his case represents another example of the ability of our CSH to bring a real impact into the lives of those here. Unfortunately, we cannot slip into thinking that we will be the answer for all of their medical needs

04 May 03 – Today is Sunday, and the day started as a cool morning under a cloudless sky. The night had been cool also, and the sleeping was good. A Steady State Brief in which we collectively briefed the commander on the workload for the month of April replaced this morning's usual staff meeting. Dave had compiled the Medicine data and briefed them to her. Overall, there were 220 admissions since we opened and 149 surgeries, with the majority of those being orthopedic, but not the eighty percent that had been forecasted. The average daily census steadily increased as the month wore on. Dave is still accumulating the acuity data, but I am convinced the average acuity of our admissions was higher than most of us expected. At times it was nothing unusual to have 5–10 patients on ventilators and pressure drips to sustain life. The average length of stay for US soldiers was barely over twenty-four hours, with most of them being evacuated within twelve hours. The length of stay for the Iraqi patients in most cases exceeded the seven-day holding capability recommended for a CSH.

The commander reported that the current inpatient census for the two slices of the 21st CSH located north of Baghdad was 13 and three, respectively. We currently stand at 28 beds occupied out of a possible 62 beds. We were able to transfer eight patients to one of the Baghdad hospitals yesterday to help lighten our load. The bottom line was that the commander was very pleased by the data and praised the department leaders for the work their sections had done. She instructed us to disseminate that out to our respective departments. I wish she would get out more and tell people in person.

We had the pleasure this morning of attending church in the newly constructed chapel, which is a seven-section temper tent similar to the rest of the hospital. It is significant because we had been having our worship service in a different location each week, none of which had chairs or air-conditioning. The new chapel has both and will be designated as a place of worship 24/7 without having to share or serve any dual roles. Chaplain C. has done an outstanding job of making things happen and continuing to minister and shepherd his flock. We now have several service opportunities each week: a Catholic Mass on Sunday mornings, a Protestant (Baptist) Worship on Sunday mornings and evenings, a mid-week prayer service, and a Bible Study on Friday evenings. There are also some other smaller groups that I have seen having Bible study on other nights. Overall, I am somewhat amazed at the spiritual situation found here in our CSH. I cannot judge people's hearts, but outwardly, the services are fairly well attended. More importantly for me, God is providing ample opportunities for me to grow spiritually here.

06 May 03 – Yesterday was the 3rd anniversary of my father's death. I spent a good deal of time thinking about him and his impact on my life. His involvement was not obvious in the classical father-son sense, but I give him credit for many things that have happened in my life and some of the better character traits I have. I certainly feel his belief in the overall good of the human spirit was genetically imparted in me. I have also inherited his open display of emotions. While that trait still makes me uncomfortable at times, I am coming to better terms with it in my "older" age.

The little boy with Giardiasis is eating everything in sight without problems, except his blood sugars remain fairly high, and we are escalating his dose of insulin. Yesterday I gave him a stuffed teddy bear that had been sent to me by Paige B. I hope she doesn't mind me sharing it with him; his eyes literally lit up when he saw me take it out of the box. It is red, white, and blue in design and has a

USA on the chest. We have been told we cannot display any American flags outdoors or in the hospital where the Iraqis can see them because we don't want to be seen as a conquering force. Seeing him with that bear is my little form of revenge against that policy, plus it really made his face brighten.

It is now in the mid to upper 90's during the days and 60's at night. We are expecting two more days of shamals starting late tomorrow. I collected sand in the miniature Tabasco bottles today for my kids.

07 May 03 – Last night we were treated to a genuine outdoor movie experience, compliments of the 207th Neurosurgery Team that joined us recently. Being a small element of less than 20 personnel, they are able to travel much better than the larger CSH. That means that while we are envious of their nicer Temper tent and the fact that they have their own ECU (air-conditioning unit), we have benefited from the other "creature comforts" they were able to bring along. One of their comforts was a projector, which they rapidly connected to a DVD player. They added some decent speakers and an eight by ten foot wooden frame, which was then covered with a sheet to make an instant outdoor theater that they have named, "The Desert Oasis Drive-In."

It is actually a walk-in with some bench seats, but there is plenty of room to add a folding camp chair, which everyone seems to have. Last night we watched "We Were Soldiers Once . . . and Young," which was especially moving, given the circumstances we are in. An added degree of authenticity occurred when several minutes of dialogue was drowned out by the sounds of med-evac helicopters landing and taking off here. The net effect of the theater under the moon and stars was breathtaking for me. I look forward to many more evening features in that little oasis.

08 May 03 – The shamal came in last evening as predicted and wasn't too bad by our standards to this point. We were able to close the tent flaps down and secure the doors fairly well. The coating of dust on our bodies and our stuff this morning was really minimal. Due to the winds, there was no film last night at The Oasis Drive-In – I think I incorrectly called it the Desert Oasis in my prior

entry. By either name it is a diamond in these rough surroundings. The morning was more breezy than usual, and the shamal has actually persisted throughout today, but at least the wind kept the temperature down a little more than usual.

Bill and I feel we made cardiology history this morning when we performed the first ever dobutamine stress echocardiogram test in a combat zone. Simply said, we infused a medication into the patient's IV that made his heart speed up and simulate an exercises stress test, all the while monitoring his EKG and obtaining echocardiogram images of his heart working. The patient was a special interest Iraqi man who Bill admitted with chest pain yesterday. We felt that he was the perfect candidate to perform this test on and identify any high-risk findings for the presence of coronary artery disease.

The test went well, both for the patient and us, and we were able to define him as low risk for having significant disease. After that, Bill was able to transfer him back to the holding facility with advice for treatment of his hypertension. We have the whole procedure recorded and plan to write the process up and submit it as a case report about diagnostic cardiac testing in a war zone. I joked with the commander the other day that if we keep up this pace of cardiology testing she would have to find us a catheterization lab before long.

09 May 03 – Our newest staff member, Rick B., started work this morning as our pediatrician. He comes to work with us just in time, as our pediatric census grew from two to nine patients during my call period yesterday. He seems happy to be here and will be allowed to return home with his unit (549th ASMC) if they redeploy before us. In the meantime, he'll be our daytime pediatrician to assist us in the management of all these ill children. The medicine staff will continue to pull the night call and get Rick's assistance the next morning on any children admitted. I feel relieved already.

10 May 03 – The day ended yesterday in a nice fashion with the showing of "When Harry Met Sally" at the Oasis drive-in. That movie continues to be one of my favorite relationship movies because it brings back memories of the fall of 1989 when it

came out and Ana and I were in the initial stages of our friendship/ romance/marriage. I still remember the theater in Miami where we watched it together.

(As I finished writing the last sentence our S3 [operations officer] came into the flea bag and said she needed me to go to Baghdad to evaluate a very high profile four-month-old infant with a heart condition).

When the S3 came in, I was sitting and talking with Rick B. our new pediatrician. I immediately said that I needed him to go with me because infants with heart problems often have other medical issues that need to be addressed. She agreed and told us we had 15 minutes to prepare to leave. As scheduled, a Blackhawk landed around 1400 local time to carry us into Baghdad. When we boarded the aircraft, the pilot asked us if we knew our destination. When I said no, he said that they had a grid coordinate, but it was a little unusual. We lifted off for the quick flight into the city and landed on a strip of dirt that was near what appeared to be one of the famous palaces. The reason the pilot thought things were unusual was that we had flown to 5th Corps Headquarters, which has been the command and control for the war effort. There we were introduced to the Corps Surgeon, who was a family physician, and he briefed us about the situation.

We then met a British major who worked for the two-star British general who was in charge of the humanitarian effort for CFLCC (Coalition Forces Land Component Command). The major further briefed us that a certain four-month-old Iraqi girl had captured the attention of the 2nd highest political figure in Great Britain (behind the Prime Minister) via a segment he'd seen televised on the BBC. They had reported that this girl was ill and had been diagnosed with a heart defect. This politician had apparently lost a daughter who had died from a similar ailment. He had instructed the British military structure that he wanted this girl transferred out of Iraq for surgical treatment.

Our role was to assess her ability to make the flight. We left the 5th Corp HQ with the British group and traveled to the British Embassy to meet up with reporters from the BBC who were coordinating the possible evacuation of this girl through a British charitable organization called Chain of Hope. We traveled in small SUV's that were relatively unassuming to avoid calling attention to our convoy. In spite of all the recent accidents and sniper incidents in Baghdad, I did not feel unsafe today while traveling in the city. I think the biggest reason for this is that I gave it all up to God for our safety prior to leaving. I believe in His protection according to His will, especially if we are acting in a humanitarian effort.

After meeting the reporting crew at the embassy, we moved by convoy over to the Kadissia General Hospital in what had been called Saddam City. It is on the northeast side of Baghdad and is considered one of the poorer areas of town. It is also reported to be the most non-secure section. At the hospital we met with the pediatrician caring for the girl. He was an older Iraqi physician who had received some training at English-speaking hospitals years ago because his English was quite good. He escorted us to the pediatric area, which housed at least fifty more children in somewhat crowded conditions with no monitoring. At the bedside he introduced us to her parents and formally presented her case to us. All the while, the camera was filming the story for the BBC.

Briefly, she was roughly 4 months old and had been brought to them 10 days ago for problems with eating and failure to thrive. She was extremely tiny, weighing less than 4 kg (9 lbs.) and had a weak cry. She had a small IV catheter in her left hand. She did not have good skin color. He showed us an X-ray from admission with an enlarged heart and hazy lung fields, followed by an X-ray from two days prior that showed marked improvement. He stated that she was in congestive heart failure on arrival and had improved with lasix and digoxin, as well as antibiotics for a presumed pneumonia. They also showed us an echocardiogram report, which listed her diagnosis as "ventral septal defect."

I asked permission to perform an echocardiogram for them to see. In spite of my limits of skill in performing a pediatric echo, it was clear that she had some complex cardiac birth defect and would benefit from any advanced care that she could get.

The BBC reporters then had us speak by satellite phone with

a cardiothoracic surgeon in the UK to give an assessment of her condition. Upon completing this step, we returned to the British Embassy, talked some more with the reporters, and then returned to the HQ area.

I snapped many photos that I hope turn out. The city seems to be returning to normal, although I think it is hard to tell what normal really is. There are signs of the war and the bombings, but these areas seem to be confined to certain buildings. There is much about Baghdad that speaks more about economic sanctions and repressive governments than it does about damage from war. Many areas were filthy with trash in the streets. My own personal comparison would be to someplace like West Africa, which I visited on a mission trip in 1987. It was evident that looting had taken place, but people and traffic seemed to be returning to normal, although there were no working traffic lights.

The hospital itself was older and run down, but not filthy by any means. It had been spared from looting by the people of the neighborhood who had organized and were patrolling the building and grounds and turning away any one who seemed intent on making trouble. There were no weapons visible, but everyone entering was searched and instructed about appropriate behavior.

Back at CFLCC we were taken into the palace to meet the British two-star general who is tasked with coordinating this mission. The palace was one of many that Saddam had in the Baghdad area. If I wrote several pages I would not come close in describing the opulence of this palace. I only hope my pictures come out reasonably well. The ceilings were at least 12–15 feet high in every room, and the entire floor and walls that I saw were made of marble. Chandelier lighting and gold plating was everywhere. This particular palace had suffered only minor damage. For me, the culmination of the high adventure of today's trip was when I sat with the British General in one of the lavish bedrooms of the palace having tea. I can easily say that I never would have imagined that scenario. It is the kind of thing I'll tell stories about for many years.

Back at the CSH, Rick and I talked about the implications of all the resources being spent on this one little girl and the amount of good it would do to be spread evenly amongst the other children. Intellectually it is the needs of the one versus the needs of the many. For now, the spotlight is directly upon this little girl, and she should probably take advantage of the opportunity to have life-saving surgery. With our recommendations, the British will now coordinate her trip and may utilize some Army assets, but it is unlikely to be us.

12 May 04 – Bill and I attended church yesterday morning and were treated to a fine message on Mother's Day. I think most folks around here were able to send flowers or gifts via the Internet to their wives and mothers. I took pleasure in writing messages to my mother-in-law Maria, to my friend Lori B., and a long letter to Ana. Even though she was on call this weekend, she said in her e-mail today that she had a wonderful Mother's Day and was helped out by my aunt Helen, her husband, Paul, and my cousin Lynn. I am deeply grateful to our family and friends who have joined forces to assist Ana while I am away in this paradise location.

All in all, life is nearly identical here on a daily basis, and some people have mentioned that it is difficult to keep the days of the week straight. I don't suffer from that problem because I use the Daily Bread devotional series for my morning Bible reading and that always keeps me oriented.

15 May 03 – One of the many problems with us now sending the original 32-bed package forward is that much of the intended equipment was used to establish this hospital, and the remainder of our hospital is back in Kuwait at Camp Victory. We are reverting to the original plan for determining how many providers to send. There will be two surgeons, one orthopedist, one anesthesiologist, two Certified Registered Nurse Anesthetists (CRNA)'s, one emergency physician, one family physician, and me. I am not sure about the number of nurses or other ancillary support staff. I had been chosen to be part of the original 32-bed package, and Bill and I talked and decided that nothing had changed that should alter that original plan. We felt it was important to send one of us and leave one of us here, given that we were the only two critical care physicians for the CSH. Needless to say, I am not pleased about breaking

up our partnership, both on a personal and professional level. Bill and I have grown much closer as a result of this insanity others call the 28th CSH.

16 May 03 – This morning Bill, Chris, and I went outside where we found the convoy lining up to take Dave and others back to Kuwait. Dave is carrying a small package back to Ana and the kids for me. We exchanged bittersweet farewells and came inside the DFAC to have a breakfast of cereal, milk, fruit, and coffee. Every one of us out here would have jumped at the opportunity to be in the back of that truck, but we are happy for our friends.

The commander announced at the staff meeting today that the 32-bed package is to depart on Tuesday for the trip to Tikrit. That is four days away, and I don't realistically see how that can happen. There are still too many things that have to fall in place in perfect order to make us mission capable, and I'm skeptical that things will be ready.

18 May 03 – It is Sunday after the morning worship service, and the message for me today was a challenge to persevere and to allow God to call "my cadence," with a scriptural reference to Isaiah 40 that encourages us to soar with the presence of God and complete the race before us. The timing of the message could not be any better. Yesterday was a tough day, with thoughts of leaving here and moving again. Things were beginning to wind down last evening until the winds kicked up and another shamal came through, wreaking havoc on our tents and on my spirit. I ended up coming back into the hospital to sleep in our call room because I just could not mentally deal with another night of being coated with dust. I attempted to call home again last night and actually connected, but was only able to leave a message on the machine.

The chapel will be taken down to provide tents for the Tikrit mission. I have been told that the DFAC dining tent will also come down. As far as I am concerned, these two structures are key aspects of the spiritual and physical morale of our CSH, and their absence will be disheartening for the short term. I only hope that they are replaced as soon as the supplies come up from the rear.

19 May 03 – Today is Ana's birthday, and it just reminds me

of another significant event occurring in my life that I am not able to take part in because I am here. We have been away from home for almost ten weeks now, and I think it is getting harder instead of easier. I was finally able to speak to her early this morning, which was around 10:30 in the evening for her. I ended up using one of the satellite phones because I was unable to get through on the Army phone. I threw myself on the mercy of the staff members in the tactical operations center (TOC) and felt somewhat disappointed that I had to feel guilty about doing so. I was careful not to abuse the privilege and only spoke for 5 minutes, but it was very good to hear her voice.

Midway through the afternoon, the commander came by to tell us that we were not leaving in the morning; the movement has been delayed for an indefinite period of time. The staking party will proceed up to Tikrit tomorrow, and several of the milvans containing most of our stuff have already been moved north, as per plans. That leaves me with my rucksack that, fortunately, contains most of my clothes and toiletries. It seems as if I have learned something about being prepared from being on this deployment.

21 May 03 – The motivation to eagerly arise each morning is becoming harder here. The monotony is becoming more apparent. Waves of apathy seem to roll over me, not unlike the waves of the ocean reaching the shore. After a while, the tide goes back out, and I am able to get up and do something productive. The US soldiers continue to be evacuated backwards to the 47th CSH in Kuwait City and then back to Landstuhl, Germany, if appropriate.

Yesterday we transferred four burn patients to a hospital in the United Arab Emirates. I am not sure how this deal was arranged, but it was similar to the one we had several weeks ago for the adult woman who went to Saudi Arabia. The political dynamics here have been challenging because we have had difficulty transferring any Iraqi citizens out of Iraq, especially to Kuwait. The Kuwaiti Health Ministry has apparently offered to accept Iraqi children, but the Defense Ministry has prevented this from happening. The situation blends in perfectly with the animosity that certain Arabs feel against other Arabs and the delay in the Iraqi healthcare system being fully operational again. I really believe if they could handle more of their own healthcare mission, our work here would dwindle and we would be able to come home sooner rather than later.

The remaining members of our CSH arrived the other night from Camp Victory and will comprise the bulk of the personnel for the 32-bed package. I do feel badly for them because they have spent the majority of their time at Camp Victory instead of here, working in the hospital. It would be a terrible feeling to come all this way for the war and never even enter Iraq. In fact, they had been told on one day that there was no mission for them and they would be redeploying, only to be told the next day that the plans had changed. The rest of the CSH is now here and includes more nurses, techs, and the other chaplain, John K., who will initially go forward to Tikrit with us and then may return here to replace Keith when he leaves.

22 May 03 — It was amazing how hot it still felt at 2300. The sand seemed to be radiating heat, just like on a hot day at the beach. The skies were also overcast and probably holding the heat on the ground. After dusting my cot and sleeping bag off, I stripped down to the basics and lay down to sleep. It wasn't long until the wind picked up again and I found myself imagining that I was lying on the beach with the breeze blowing sand over my body. Only the ocean was nowhere to be found. I wrapped my shirt around my head hoping that I could keep one part of my body from being covered with dust in the morning. Sleep finally came, and I awoke on top of my damp sleeping bag with the usual dusting to contend with. Baby wipes are reasonably good at knocking the upper layer of dust off until the next shower time arrives.

The heat continues to be a major issue for any details or duties planned outside. I saw a note in the TOC today that yesterday was the 11th consecutive day of heat greater than 100 degrees, and I am sure that trend is in no danger of ending. The heat and humidity are also affecting other aspects of daily life here, such as using the latrine. Not to belabor the point, but the smells associated with latrine use are made worse when the weather is hot and the atmosphere is stagnant. Mixed in with the smell of the latrines is the odor from the jet fuel we use to reduce the number of flies and to facilitate the burning process that must be done when the barrels become full. Those smells are certainly one thing that none of us are growing used to, and I hope we never do.

As of today we used up our supply of bottled water and must now rely upon the water buffalos for our drinking source. There is one redeeming feature to that situation in that the water in our buffalos is processed water taken from the Euphrates River, so we are drinking water from the same source as Abraham did.

24 May 03 – Lee S., our Executive Officer, came to me last night and told me my promotion sequence number had come up on the list they received, and I should plan on being promoted after the 1st of June. I told him that I would like to be promoted here, but that I wanted to make the decision about when and where and who would pin on my new rank. He said none of those things should be a problem and that he'd keep the commander informed. My date of rank is 14 June, and Medical Corp promotions usually occur on the date of rank. Lee said we could really do it anytime after the 1st of the month that I wanted. I may move it up sooner than my date of rank if it looks like we will be leaving for Tikrit before then because I want Bill to pin on the rank for me. He is the closest thing to family I have here.

I had a pleasant, long talk with Keith C. this afternoon in the fleabag. I have really grown to love him as a Christian brother, and he has had a tremendous influence on my spiritual life here. He is practicing a good brand of Christian realism that I aspire to do. I am saddened to think about him leaving in the next few weeks, but I am happy for him and the fact that he has PCS orders that will take him and his family to Japan.

25 May 03 – Over time, our congregation has slowly formed a choir for the services. Today their sound was more uplifting than ever. With the addition of the last group from Camp Victory, we had nearly 80 people in worship and included a choir of 10 people. The choir contains people with obvious musical talent, and those talents are showing through with solos and group singing. Keith's sermon was inspirational and practical, as always. Following wor-

ship, we returned to the air-conditioning of the PLX corridor in the hospital for a Bible study about "The Bible and Iraq," given by John K. He gave an overview that I will summarize here.

Genesis 2:10–14 tells of the four rivers that originated from the Garden of Eden with the Tigris and Euphrates being the two recognizable today. The outcome of the other two rivers is not known. The area between the rivers is known as Mesopotamia, or the "cradle of civilization," where we think written language began. The more generalized term "the Fertile Crescent" refers to the path that is formed from the Persian Gulf along the two rivers toward the north into Turkey and then back southward toward Israel. This arcing pathway was followed by anyone traveling from this region to the promised land of Canaan. We spent our first night in Iraq at an airfield near Tallil, which is near Ur, mentioned in Genesis 11:26–31 as the birthplace of Abram, who was later to become Abraham. This Scripture also mentions that Abram traveled north to Haran (now known as Harran), which is in northern Iraq or Turkey and is the area Abram settled in before the Lord directed him on to Canaan.

Genesis 11:1–9 mentions the Tower of Babel, whose ruins are thought to be approximately 30 miles from here. It was here that the city of Babylonia and the Babylonian Empire were built. Most notable of biblical figures in Babylon was the story of Daniel, who was held captive there. The Babylonians were responsible for the destruction of the Temple in Israel through the hands of King Nebuchadnezzar. The city of Nineveh, which Jonah was avoiding, is located across the Tigris River from the city of Mosul in northern Iraq and was the capital of Assyria. The Assyrians are felt to be the original terrorists in their methods of conquest and war fighting. Baghdad was not developed as a city of any real size until the 7th Century following the Muslim crusades. And finally, Kuwait, where we entered our adventure, was underwater during early times and was only later created by the sedimentary deposits of the Tigris and Euphrates Rivers.

26 May 03 – Today is Memorial Day here, but there is no outward evidence of celebration of this holiday, other than that we are

scheduled to have a hot meal for dinner tonight at the DFAC in addition to having had a hot breakfast. Two convoys left today: one carrying patients to a Baghdad hospital and the other going to Tallil to pick up needed items from the 86th CSH, which is redeploying. That second convoy isn't likely to return for two days, and then all the items must be assembled onto a new convoy that would proceed north.

27 May 03 – Yesterday the commander attended a meeting in Baghdad with other CSH commanders, medical brigade commanders, and Iraqi officials from the Ministry of Health. They apparently discussed many issues about current and future situations that we are all facing. She reported that we face the challenge of winning the hearts and minds of the Iraqi people in the setting of years of them viewing us as evil people. The difficulty in managing the Shiite Muslim population was not effectively anticipated. The issue of charging for medical supplies and medical services by the Iraqi facilities has not been adequately resolved. Many Iraqi hospitals face the problem of water sanitation and not having reliable power sources. There are reported to be over 250 hospitals in Iraq and over 2000 smaller clinics. The majority of these medical facilities are not functioning at anywhere near optimum ability because of the problems mentioned above.

We then discussed the Tikrit mission and learned that we would be delayed at least until 01 June because the 86th CSH is not able to give the requested generators and cables to our convoy because they are still operational until then. I do miss my duffle bags with all my comfort items, but at least I have the rucksack that contains my clothes.

28 May 03 – I am on call again and have admitted only four patients to the medical team, but the surgeons have admitted several Iraqi burn patients and one US burn patient. Our designated burn unit is beginning to fill up again, but we are limited by the inability to care for too many patients on ventilators at one time and by the lack of a dermatome, which would allow for skin grafting. The surgeons have stated that having the dermatome would allow for more definitive management but would also prolong the patient's stay

and draw more heavily upon our resources, such as blood products and supplies. We have been given the burn center mission without the full support of the supply system. We were all worried this exact thing would happen.

An Iraqi patient with kidney failure continues to do poorly and is in need of dialysis. As of this afternoon, our civil affairs people have arranged for him to be transferred to a Baghdad hospital in the morning. On a lighter note, the s4 (staff officer responsible for logistics and supply) ordered several copies of the Harriet Lane Handbook for pediatrics, and they have arrived. The problem is that they are written in Spanish. That slight oversight speaks volumes about the challenges we have faced with logistics on this deployment.

30 May 03 – Another shamal is approaching, and the dust in the air at sunset has had the effect of casting an unearthly red glow to the air. I literally feel as if I am on Mars. Bill and Chris have taken pictures of the atmosphere, and I only hope they can turn out. We really despise this place and want to leave as soon as possible. I don't think I can muster the resolve to go back to the hooch in the midst of this storm. I am not on call but will likely spend the night here in the fleabag, sleeping on the floor if that becomes necessary.

01 Jun 03 – I woke up this morning with no small degree of excitement as I looked forward to my promotion to the rank of Lieutenant Colonel. The ceremony was held at 0730 outside the front entrance to the hospital near the EMT section. Although not everyone was able to attend because of patient care duties, there were several people present, and the weather was pleasant with a lower temperature and a slight breeze. The backdrop for the ceremony was the desert landscape with several ambulances and the communication vehicles. COL P. spoke about my biographical information and had some complementary comments about my role in the hospital and as a department chief. Then she and Bill removed the Major's rank from my collar and replaced it with that of Lieutenant Colonel. After prior warning, Bill then saluted me, a gesture that I found particularly moving because of our friendship that has been made even closer by this deployment.

In proper tradition, I then held the floor for remarks. I had given some thought to my comments and admitted as much to the group. I spoke of two things that stand out in my mind in regards to this promotion. First, I thought of being a poor graduate student at Wake Forest in 1988 and needing to finance my medical school education. I was easily convinced to become a scholarship merce- nary for the US Army, but I had no idea that decision would lead me to meet my wife at the Officer Basic Course (OBC) in the summer of 1989 in San Antonio, nor did I have any idea that I'd still be in the Army in 2003. Looking into the audience I was also reminded of MAJ Mark W., who is our Patient Affairs Officer here, who was then my OBC class leader. I fondly pointed out to the group this morn- ing that Mark has mellowed considerably since his days as a second Lieutenant who was trying to manage a group of spoiled medical students from all across the country.

Second, I explained how I had turned age 40 in December 2002 prior to learning of this deployment and how I had thought to myself that I wanted something truly significant to happen in my life during this year. There is little way that I could have predicted the events I am experiencing here. I have been giving more thought lately to the significance of this deployment in my life. I have already documented that I believe the primary reason for me being here is to grow my relationship with God. Expanding on that premise, I also believe that in fostering that relationship I will learn a new appre- ciation for the things in my life that are important – my wife, my children, my other family members, and my friends. I won't avoid the fact that things that I consider as comforts are also important, but I have been reminded that I could do without them should the need arise. I won't go so far as to say that I am happy here because I am separated from my wife and children, but I continually strive to be content in the circumstances, knowing that it is in God's perfect will that I am here.

In a recent e-mail from a friend in Fayetteville, I was reminded that I am also here because God has blessed me with an under- standing of human illness and an ability to intervene in that illness. While I am often outside my personal comfort zone of medical practice here, I fully realize that I am still considered a fairly accomplished practitioner of medicine to the Iraqis.

02 Jun 03 – Yesterday ended pleasantly with mild temperatures and several of us sitting outside the sleep tents talking about life on the deployment and what it was going to be like when we return home. We went around the circle and answered the question, "Where would you go with your spouse for a four day escape?" There were varied responses, but I am leaning toward a posh resort at a nice beach where Ana and I can be seriously pampered and spoiled. Conventional logic would say that I would be sick of sand by that time, but I realize that this place is not the real world and that in most places there cannot be an area of sand wider than 30 or 40 yards that doesn't have a large body of water attached to it. I long for the sound of the waves lapping against the shoreline to wipe the sights, smells, and sounds of this place away.

We concluded that the biggest obstacle to sanity right now for us is the uncertainty that comes with having no firm endpoint in sight. I think we could even be coping better if we knew that we wouldn't be home until November or December. I don't think that any of us believe we'll be here that long, but without a date to plan for, we are left to toil along without an objective. The days are all so similar here; it is very difficult to recognize a Monday from a Saturday.

Several of the pediatric patients are still here, and the newest admission to our children's hospital was an 18-month-old girl who has some form of skin disorder that causes widespread sloughing of the skin and mucous membranes. In its severest form, which this little girl appears to have, it is universally fatal by age three or four. The management calls for supportive care and genetic counseling for the parents, instructing them that they have a 25% chance of each child they bear having this disorder. We have, unfortunately, seen many pitiful appearing children while on this deployment, but she may be the worst of all.

Lately, the illnesses I see in these children have been more difficult for me to accept because my thoughts drift to my own children. There is a reason God did not lead me into pediatrics. I have the utmost respect for physicians like my wife who are gifted in this specialty. I wish that she were here to help us treat these children.

03 Jun 03 - There has been a definite excitement in the air today because it appears that we are really moving out to Tikrit tomorrow. I spent most of the day visiting different areas of the hospital and saying my farewells to the folks who are not traveling north. The toughest person to say farewell to has been Bill, but then again, we don't really need to say farewell to one another because this deployment will not be the end for us.

We received a formal convoy briefing at 1930. The revised plan has us waking at 0300 to get ready for a final manifest or roll call at 0400 and moving out at 0500. We were given our truck assignments and should be crowding about 14 bodies into the backs of the five-tons for the planned six hour ride. I have successfully packed everything up and will sleep in the fleabag tonight.

After the convoy briefing, we held as near to a real going away party as we could muster in the desert in these conditions. SSG T., one of the surgery non-commissioned officers, hosted the celebration near his tent, and it included chips and salsa, music, and some people who were actually dancing. We kept the reverie going until almost midnight, and then I came back into the hospital for sleeping.

Another big news item today was that we admitted Tariq Aziz, the former deputy Prime Minister. He has a somewhat complicated cardiac history and was referred for us to evaluate episodes of nearly passing out that he has been having.

Bill and I converged on him quickly while taking his history and performing his physical examination. He was quite pleasant and fairly fluent in English. In speaking to him, we learned that he has felt poorly for several days but has been engaged in hunger strikes on and off for the past few weeks. Our overall clinical impression was that he was dehydrated and somewhat over-medicated for his conditions. We performed an echocardiogram and an electrocardiogram. We made some adjustments to his medications, and I made sure that Bill and Chris and I had extra copies of his EKG with his name on it as a sort of cardiology wartime souvenir.

6 / The Convoy to Tikrit

04 Jun 03 – We awoke before 0400, loaded the few remaining items, and said our good-byes to our fellow soldiers and friends. The planned starting time was 0500, but as usual for the 28ᵗʰ, we ended up pulling out of the compound shortly before 0600. Our departure was accompanied, again, by a group salute similar to the one we had received upon leaving Camp Victory – only this time there was no US flag. We had only rolled a short distance off the FLB Dogwood compound when we stopped for an equipment break-down, but we were able to move out again shortly. It turns out that this early breakdown should have been a warning sign that things were not meant to go smoothly on this convoy.

After crossing the Euphrates River, the scenery changed dra-matically to green surroundings, and we began to see many people going about their daily lives, including children walking to school and men and women walking along the roads to taxi pick-up points. The taxis here fall into two categories: small, four-door vehicles, or mini-buses that can hold 15–20 people. The people were usu-ally curious and friendly, and they waved vigorously as we passed by. Riding along on this Wednesday morning, it was almost easy to forget that we were in a hostile country during war, except for the fact that we were riding in Kevlar helmets and flak vests with magazines in our weapons, and we periodically would see "disabled" tanks along the sides of the road.

As we traveled around the western outskirts of Baghdad, I was struck by how modern much of the city appeared. Many of the neighborhoods had gates, walls, and driveways with reason-able looking cars in them. There was an abundance of palm trees and other vegetation. Interspersed with these neighborhoods were ones that were much more run down and looked like slums. All along the way, the piles of garbage and rubbish that was beside the highway impressed me. There was very limited evidence of bombing or damage from the war in the areas that we saw. We also passed by the Saudi Arabian field hospital that we had heard had been established in Baghdad. Even though its front gate was guarded, the compound appeared overflowing with people who were likely a mixture of patients and family members.

We were progressing well in the far left lane of a three-lane expressway. The drivers around us were being somewhat aggressive in their style, but none of us in my truck were prepared for the accident involving the 5-ton truck immediately behind us. Upon hearing a commotion I turned in time to see the truck swerve sharply to its left and proceed over the 8-inch median divider and into the oncoming lanes of traffic on the other side. The truck fish-tailed severely but remained upright, much in part to the milvan that it was towing, which acted as a stabilizing force to keep it from becoming airborne after jumping over the median.

The three occupants of the truck cab and the 12 soldiers in the cargo area were literally thrown around, but sustained no fractures or life-threatening injuries. The truck struck two cars and one van on the opposite side of the road, but there were no injuries, and only the van was incapable of driving away from the accident. In the process of jumping the median, the dolly set carrying the milvan exploded three of its four tires, and the truck exploded an additional four tires. Needless to say, after we caught our collective breath, the convoy pulled to the right side of the highway and waited while the tires were changed, a process that took over 2 and ½ hours. Although we were literally stopped beside a trash dump, none of us were complaining, as we realized the severity of the situation. I know I privately and publicly gave thanks to God for providing angelic protection upon all those involved in the crash.

When the repairs were completed, our security escort blocked all six lanes of north and southbound traffic while our truck rejoined the remainder of the 20-vehicle convoy on our side of the road. Back underway again, we traveled without major mechanical incident but did miss one exit that required a u-turn several miles later. The remainder of the ride was quite uncomfortable because of the temperature and hard seats. Sleep was impossible, and my rear became numb after a while from the hardness of the bench and the bounces caused by the poor truck suspension over bumpy roads. After traveling more than five hours more, we reached Camp Speicher at Tikrit North around 1630, completing the convoy in about 10 hours, when it was supposed to take six hours.

Camp Speicher is located at the former Iraqi Air Force Academy and is named after Navy Captain Michael Scott Speicher who piloted an F-18 Hornet during the Gulf War in 1991. The Air Force Academy has not been active since the prior desert war. We have come here because Tikrit is the site of the 4th ID headquarters, and they are requesting a hospital to support their troops. After an MRE meal enjoyed with a wonderful sunset, I collapsed from exhaustion and dehydration into my cot.

05 Jun 03 – I slept late until around 0800 and awoke still dehydrated. The temperature was already hot, and the shade from the previous afternoon was gone, as the sun was approaching from a different angle. There was, however, a nice breeze, and I found more shade underneath the concrete bleachers of the old stadium next to which we had parked our convoy. Due to the damage sustained from coalition bombing the stadium reminds me of the ruins of an ancient coliseum. I am not sure if this damage occurred during the prior or current conflict. The field is still mostly intact, although overgrown, and there are fuel pods and what appear to be warheads stored underneath the bleachers.

The landscape is different here and reminds me most of south-central Texas with scrub brush, short trees, and brown grass. The city of Tikrit is about five miles off to our southeast, and the land is rather flat with some gently rolling contour. We have also heard several birds, and one is flying over the stadium and screeching at us as if we have disturbed its territory.

I am having flashbacks to the first convoy that brought us out of Kuwait to our first hospital location. We have become cats again; I am resting, reading, writing, and drinking, with very little appetite for food. John K., our chaplain, led several of us in prayer and worship at 0900, and it was very timely for me. My mood is low, and I find myself relying upon God very strongly again for sustainment.

The group of physicians on this trip includes John L. and Cal M. as surgeons, Rob D. as urologist, Rob G. as orthopedist, Drew K. as ER physician, Fred B. as Family Physician/ER physician, and Colin G. as our DCCS or Deputy Commander for Clinical Services.

At 1800 we were told to pack up, and we moved across the airfield to the apron on the other side. The staking team was busy at work, laying out the hospital as night fell. I feel some joy as I look in the distance to our northeast and see a ridgeline appearing above the land. Having grown up in the mountains of North Carolina, being closer to any mountains at this point is a small comfort for me, even if the mountains are in Iraq.

7 / Establishing 28CSH-Tikrit

06 Jun 03 – The first sergeant (1SG) awoke us at 0500 this morning for formation and to go over the details of the formal hospital setup. We were divided into teams to set up hospital tents, water, electrical, and sleep tents. Initially we filled sandbags until 0730. We literally filled thousands because they are going to be used to pack around the tents for support. By setting the hospital onto the concrete apron beside the taxiway, we are unable to drive any stakes into the ground. Without stakes we cannot secure the ropes in the conventional way, which necessitates us lining sandbags around the base of all the tents and stacking those three high. Needless to say, that requires a lot of sandbags. I just wonder about the logic of employing the most highly trained members of the medical staff to be part of the detail.

The big difference between the hospital at Dogwood and the one here is that we do not need to install the chemical protective liner here, which saves a big step. We worked all day and took frequent breaks. The temperature was hot, but there was a nice breeze blowing, which helped to keep things bearable. Nonetheless, in spite of drinking plenty of fluids, I urinated only once the whole day.

07 Jun 03 – We awoke shortly before 0530 this morning and went to formation, only to be chewed out by the 1SG for being slackers and not getting up on time. It really was the absolute last thing I wanted to hear this morning, given my attitude toward Army life. We then returned to the dirt pile, where we filled several thousand more sandbags. After breakfast we resumed the hospital construction, but our progress was slowed by the oppressive temperature and lack of a breeze. I felt hot and weak all day, with very little urine production in spite of drinking several liters of fluid. I

carefully rationed my time in the sun and took several rest breaks. I made it successfully through the day, and by 1800 we were complete enough to turn the power on. The air-conditioning felt wonderful, and I enjoyed my MRE inside prior to a briefing from the commander at 1900. As evening fell, I rode the five-ton convoy over to the 1st Med Bde showers and returned refreshed and ready for another night under the stars.

08 Jun 03 – We awoke and attended the 0530 formation and were all on time today. We again filled thousands of sandbags before breakfast. Cal and I had arranged to go at a more comfortable pace this morning because I was still worn out and his hands were sore, which is somewhat of a livelihood issue for a surgeon. After breakfast we moved into the hospital to complete the set-up and make ready to open our doors. At 0900 we held our first worship service in the sick call tent that is attached to the EMT section. John K. led a wonderful service in celebration of the Day of Pentecost, which many consider the true birth of the church. Pentecost is mentioned in the Old Testament as the Festival of Weeks that comes seven weeks after the Passover. The group of believers here comes from many religious backgrounds, and I think we will struggle for adequate space for worship and Bible study because even though the commander's words speak of her commitment to spiritual health, her actions speak of her true feelings.

Around 2000 the commander and DCCS came through each section to perform the required inspection to verify that we were capable of accepting patients. She informed her higher headquarters that as of 2100 we were open for business. Within 15 minutes the first helicopter landed, bringing a soldier who had sustained damage to his hand in an accident. If you build it, they will come. I retired down the hill to our sleep area, which for now is even less desirable than the one we had at Dogwood because it is dusty from the dirt and has no flooring or power. Nonetheless, I went there at around 2200 and easily fell asleep.

09 Jun 03 – Today began as a normal day without the insanity of the recent formations. I awoke without prompting at around 0600 and came to the hospital to find coffee. There I learned that

my first admission had been around 2300 from the night before and was a 43-year-old master sergeant that was admitted for chest pain. I was happy to be doing clinical medicine again, but my mood is still down, and I am not as excited about starting fresh with this new hospital as I was before. The past few days have been difficult in terms of tolerating the weather, the uncertainties of us being here, and missing my family, not to mention the friends I have back at Dogwood.

I was able to use the satellite phone yesterday afternoon at the PX (which will officially open this Thursday the 12th), but I only reached Ana's voice mail on her cell phone. The satellite phones were being difficult to operate yesterday, and trying our home number was not successful. I may have felt somewhat better if I had talked to her, but it would not have cured things.

As expected, we are able to do some things the same way we have been doing them at Dogwood, and other things call for different solutions. We had a hot lunch today because the refrigerated cooler has broken, possibly due to the heat. It seems miserably oppressive here today, and the hospital never really cooled down. I spent most of the day sweating inside the hospital, looking for an area where I could hang out to spend my time. I have no flea bag here because there are fewer nooks and crannies that aren't already being used by this smaller hospital layout. Even the surgeons have a smaller niche in the pre-op area to call their own. We are all looking to find some space where we can get away and are out of everyone's way.

10 Jun 03 – Today has been a slow day clinically with few admissions and few visits to the ER. We have been told that the outside temperature is in the 120's, which is unworldly to me. The thermometer outside the Tactical Operations Center (TOC) shows the indicator past the 120-degree mark. The temperature inside the EMT section was 102 degrees in the middle of the afternoon. There have been several visitors over the past two days, as many physicians from the nearby medical support companies and staff members from the 1st Medical Brigade (Med Bde) have been stopping in to tour and assess our capabilities. They have all been pleasantly surprised at our location, set-up, and the specialty care that we are

offering. I have already seen three patients sent specifically for cardiology evaluations.

The DFAC dining tent is being built this evening, and we should be able to eat in there soon. For the next few days we've been told to expect a breakfast of cereal, fruit, and milk, while dinner will be our hot meal.

My mood is somewhat improved today, although by no means normal. I realize that will take time, and I will not truly feel normal until I am back with my wife and children. I think I really miss Bill and the other medical staff members that are at Dogwood. After our morning staff meeting, I visited our showers for the first time and was pleasantly surprised at what a nice structure our laundry and bath folks had put together. I miss the brick flooring that we had at Dogwood, but these showers are overall much nicer, with a larger changing area that has wood floors and benches to sit on. The flooring in the shower area is rubber and seems to drain well because of the slope. I was able to get over there just before the morning session ended and was able to enjoy it all to myself, which had never happened at Dogwood. I think there are definite advantages to being part of a 150-person hospital here versus the 500-person hospital in the latter days there at Dogwood.

Our census had risen to 10 patients, but we were able to discharge or transfer our way back down to our current census of three patients, two of which are Iraqis. The night shift nurses and staff are finding it difficult to sleep during the day due to the heat, so it is fortunate that we are not that busy until they get the dedicated sleep tents built with Environmental Control Units (ECU's) for cooling.

8 / Summer at Camp Speicher

11 Jun 03 – It has been unbelievably hot, and the heat starts rising by 0900 in the morning. I have never been so hot in my life, not in El Paso, not in San Antonio, and certainly not anywhere in North Carolina. The heat dictates everything that we do. It is nearly intolerable to be outside, and it is not even pleasant at times to be inside the so-called air-conditioned hospital. I think the outside temperature is making it difficult on the ECU's to truly cool the inside. At around noon I saw a cardiology consult in the EMT section, and the temperature read 105 degrees – inside.

Apathy doesn't even begin to describe how I feel during the day when it is so hot. I literally don't want to do anything. Walking outside to use the latrine results in profuse sweating. There are many little projects I tell myself I could be working on, but I keep procrastinating, thinking that things will cool down in a few days. The one thing I am doing a great deal of is sitting and reading. I feel really badly for the night shift because the sleep tent is not fully functional yet, and I can't imagine trying to sleep in this weather because I'd be worried about drowning in my sweat.

12 Jun 03 – The Internet has still not been wired all over the hospital yet, and I am beginning to lose patience. Currently I have to go into the TOC and use one of the staff's terminals to read and send e-mail, and I am getting tired of it. I tried the Army phones earlier this morning, but the lines out were busy for over 15 minutes. The satellite phones are supposedly going to be available to us for a few hours tonight at rates that range between 80 cents and one dollar per minute. I had tried these phones the other afternoon at the PX parking lot and had faced difficulty getting through. The grand opening of the PX is today, but no one has mentioned going.

13 Jun 03 – The night and morning were very pleasant, and then around 1130 this morning our first shamal set in and has been blowing for about the past two hours. I have not ventured outside to see how it differs, if at all, from the ones we have encountered until now. It is certainly blowing the sides of the hospital tent, and I notice that there is more dust in the air.

Our patient census is at nine this morning, with three Iraqi males who are recovering from surgery but should be able to go back to custody tomorrow or the next day. The other patients are US soldiers with a variety of diagnoses, including one patient I am following who has a chronic skin condition that has been made worse by him being in this hot, sunny environment. He is usually stationed at Ft Lewis in Washington State, and we are going to try to return him there.

I find myself doing things lately that help me escape mentally from this place. Movies and books are the easiest and most healthy things here to help me escape. I have written over the past few days about my mood, and it is still down from normal, but I had been feeling better until this morning when the shamal started. I hate these sand storms that dominate your feelings because they scatter dust over everything that you own, fill your mouth with dust, and cover your body and clothes if you happen to have the misfortune of being outside.

14 Jun 03 – Today is my official date of rank, which means that although I had pinned on the rank of LTC earlier in the month before the trip up here, it was six years ago on this date that I had been promoted to major. It is also Flag Day and the Army's Birthday, having been formed on 14 June 1775, one year prior to the formal creation of the United States.

It is after dinner now, and I am trying to decide whether to read or watch another movie. The weather is not bad outside, so I may read a while and then retire to the tent for some outside relaxation. I sure miss the Oasis Theater and the outdoor movies. I have a coating of dust at pretty much all times, except for those brief moments when I complete my shower and before I use my dust-coated towel to dry off.

15 Jun 03 – It's Father's Day here, and we started it off with a Father's Day Prayer Breakfast. John K. conducted the well-attended service and made several key points about being a Christian father. Several people shared heart-felt testimonies about what fatherhood meant to them. I would obviously rather be at home with my children on this day, but I am striving very hard to be content in my circumstances. Because our mail situation is failing me, I haven't received the Father's Day package that Ana has sent. In a bit of a role reversal, I decided to send cards to my kids and Ana and included recent digital photos of me. I know they will enjoy the images, and I hope it encourages them in my absence.

I was able to reach Ana and the kids by a satellite phone on loan from the new PX. We were able to use our calling cards to make our calls at the low rate of $1.00+ per minute. Regardless of the cost, it was wonderful to be able to hear their voices and savor them wishing me a happy Father's Day. I have noticed that as much as I try to prevent it, my mood rapidly rises and falls based on whether I am able to talk with them by phone when I make the effort and have the opportunity. I am recharged for several more days having spoken to them.

17 Jun 03 – Transferring our Iraqi patients is now the same logistical challenge we faced at Dogwood. I am guardedly optimistic that it may be easier to accomplish placement here because the chief nurse and preventative medicine officer from the 1st Med Bde rounded with us yesterday afternoon and told us that they had been building the relationship with the hospital in Tikrit. They feel that the facility is more than adequate for the types of patients that we have, and their physicians are anxious to meet us and interact in a professional manner.

It has been one of the biggest challenges of this deployment to show the love of Christ in ministering to the people who are our enemies. Most Iraqis are humble and meek and they rarely seem hostile after their arrival and appear genuinely thankful for our care. But I struggle constantly to maintain the right attitude towards them because I harbor the feeling that they have been out shooting at our soldiers or looting weapons or ammunition, either to sell as a way of buying food or to use the looted items against US soldiers. We are further handicapped at present in that we have no interpreter working for us. Our original interpreter who traveled with us from Kuwait was ultimately released last week because his attitude was so bad and his services were so inferior. The nurses have picked up some basic Arabic and can communicate about food, pain, and hygiene issues, but we are operating from a position of weakness in not being able to talk to the Iraqi patients.

Last night never cooled down to a comfortable level for sound sleeping, and I awoke with a sweat-drenched pillow and decided to go for a run. The sun was breaking over the horizon as I started, and it provided me a wonderful visual show as I slowly moved along the airstrip runway, using muscles that hadn't been required since before we deployed. I was careful not to overdo things on the first morning, and so I felt pretty good upon finishing and headed to the showers.

After showering I moved up to the DFAC tent, where there was a hot breakfast of scrambled eggs, hash browns, and grits that was quite good. After breakfast I made rounds with the other physicians and then moved on to get my work done and my notes written for the day.

Bill sounds tired on the phone down at Dogwood, and he says that the patient acuity is still high there, the weather is hot, and being on every other night call is beginning to wear him down. He stated that morale seems to be really dipping, as there is no end in sight for all of us leaving.

All of us need a break because we have been practicing medicine without a break for over 90 straight days – with the exception of the time we were on the convoy and setting up the hospital here – and it is beginning to wear us down. I have heard that during the first version of the desert war there were options provided for R&R such as an actual cruise ship in the Persian Gulf or designated resorts in Saudi Arabia.

18 Jun 03 – This morning we were visited by the 4th ID Division Surgeon, the local Civilian Affairs Physician, and several Iraqi physicians from the medical center here in Tikrit. We had been told

to expect the military physicians and were prepared to discuss disposition issues with them concerning our Iraqi patients. The arrival of the Iraqi physicians was an unexpected and well-received surprise. Most of them spoke English, some better than the rest, and had been trained in Western facilities.

They were all very professional in their demeanor and had several complimentary statements about our facilities and capabilities. They were also grateful for the care we were providing the Iraqi patients. Needless to say, it was an amazing exchange of information and experiential knowledge about the challenges faced during the conflict and in the post-conflict phase. I feel like this type of scenario is what we should have been striving for in the past 4–6 weeks at Dogwood, but we were limited by physical isolation. The upshot of our discussions about the patients, especially the three burn patients, was that they said they would gladly accept them on transfer into the medical center hospital downtown. Our challenge now is to coordinate the convoy support to be able to do this in the next few days before the patients' conditions deteriorate further. Before leaving, they suggested we transfer the father and son Iraqi patient to one of their other hospitals later today.

It's later in the day, and I have just returned from that transfer of the father and son patient to the former Iraqi military hospital that is located in north Tikrit, about 10 minutes from here. It is a single story structure that has long been neglected but is quite adequate to provide the services the Iraqi patients would need after they are stabilized here. It is rundown but generally clean, with power, water, and air-conditioned patient wards that held eight patients each.

The physician on call who met us was very cordial, spoke reasonable English, and welcomed the patients we transferred there. He accompanied us on a tour of the facility, and we learned that it had been a military hospital prior to the war and was restricted from the general public. It was not one of Saddam's elite facilities, but rather was designed for the non-high ranking service members. It has been open for 6 weeks to the public, and they have performed 37 surgical procedures in that time. It has been renamed the Saladin

Public Hospital in honor of the 13th Century Iraqi hero from Tikrit that Saddam was known to pattern himself after.

The potential capacity is over 400 patients, but they are operating at much less than that because of lack of medical supplies and equipment. What they lack in means they appear to overcome with their desire to succeed. The physician we talked to was a former military physician who was ecstatic to see the Saddam regime fall because of the inequalities in the healthcare system. He spoke confidently that the healthcare system would right itself once the government was organized and functioning. I certainly respect his desire to stand in the gap of supporting the transition of the Iraqi healthcare system. In the end, he also thanked us for the care we provided to the Iraqi patients and stated that they would happily receive any Iraqi patients on transfer.

As we returned to Camp Speicher, and I certainly felt a great deal of satisfaction about the job we are doing here. These events are somewhat rare, but on days like these I am able to look past my own personal issues and realize that we truly are here for a reason and that the work we are doing is vital to the overall nation building effort. The opportunity to interact on an intellectual and academic level with the Iraqi physicians is what we have all been looking for.

It has been windy again today, not shamal standards, but enough to stir up the dust nonetheless. I heard the best description today regarding the ubiquitous dust. One of the Iraqi physicians upon seeing a gust of wind blow some of the dust into the EMT section said that we were being properly introduced to "Iraqi flour." I cannot think of a better way to describe it.

19 Jun 03 – I arose today before sunrise, stretched my tight muscles and went for another short run. The sun was late in appearing above the haze but was again quite striking when it did. After showering, eating, and rounding, I attended the morning staff meeting where we discussed the issues that seem to be recurring problems – poor supply lines, lack of mail delivery, lack of an interpreter, and the difficulty in classifying our patients as EPW or civilian.

Trying to capitalize on the momentum that we witnessed yesterday in transferring the Iraqi patients to the local hospital, we placed a call to coordinate the transfer of the Iraqi burn patients. Surprisingly we were able to arrange the transfer for 1130 this morning. Cal, COL G., a nurse, a technician, a respiratory therapist, and I loaded into two ambulances and moved out for the Tikrit Teaching Hospital, which is located on the south end of town. The ride through downtown was interesting in that we traveled farther than we had yesterday, and we were able to see the market place and several businesses operating from storefront locations. The traffic was manageable, and the crowds were controlled. We arrived at the hospital within 30–40 minutes without incident. Several physicians and many aides, who did not appear to have formal medical training but were providing the manpower pool, met us.

The hospital itself is a six-story structure built in the 1980's by the Japanese. As a university teaching hospital under Saddam's regime, it was built to a common template and is similar to all the other university hospitals in other cities in Iraq. Like the hospital I saw yesterday, this one is in need of repairs from neglect but sustained very little damage from the conflict. It sits on the south end of the palace property, and until recently, the windows on the palace side of the building were boarded up to prevent the people from looking into the compound. The palace buildings themselves were extravagant in outward appearance, as would be expected.

While the nursing team demonstrated the dressing changes on one of the burn patients to the accepting physicians, the medical director showed several of us around the hospital. We visited the pediatric ward, the surgery ward, and the ICU. The wards were organized in the same manner, with each room capable of holding six patients. When we saw patients in the rooms, the family members were in attendance, and my impression is that there are far fewer nurses in their system and the families do the nursing care.

The facility was relatively clean and had no issues with power, water, or air-conditioning. The floors were linoleum tile, and there were functioning elevators that had obviously been built by the Japanese because of the small size. The ICU had space for six patients, and all the beds were taken. Most, but not all beds had continuous monitoring. I noticed a cardiac crash cart with a defibrillator device and an EKG machine. The ventilator systems were old but appeared functional. After the transfer of care of the patients, we posed for a group photo with all the physicians and bid them farewell. As we left, two of the Iraqi patients expressed thanks to us for taking such good care of them.

20 Jun 03 – Our new interpreter is a well-groomed man and is an unemployed physicist. I believe he said that he held a teaching post at Tikrit University, which is located not far from here but is not yet considered safe enough for classes to resume. In the meantime, he wants to spend his time being helpful to us and making some income. My limited use of him today for one patient was a significant improvement over the services I'd received from the prior interpreter who had traveled with us up from Kuwait.

21 Jun 03 – It is early evening, and we just received our second "Christmas-type" mail delivery that included numerous packages. Because of the move north we have not received mail in almost three weeks, and the morale has sagged tremendously during this time. I received six packages and three letters that had been mailed at various times during the deployment. The biggest highlight from the packages were the pictures that Ana sent in a Father's Day gift. The pictures chronicled our years together as parents. I definitely shed some tears as I looked at them and recalled the emotions they created at the time.

22 Jun 03 – I was challenged by the chaplain in worship today to truly understand what faith meant to me and how it was holding up as the days pass by. The timing of the message was perfect because I think many of us are wondering if the end of this deployment will ever come. Yesterday was a fantastic day, with everyone connecting to home through the packages and letters. It doesn't take long, however, for the excitement to be replaced by sadness as we think about being away from our families and friends. It's definitely one of those bittersweet moments like when we get to actually talk on the phone to loved ones; it is great at the moment, but soon you realize how much you miss being there, and you get frustrated that things here seem to be dragging on.

The scripture today was from Mark 9 and it demonstrates how hopeless a situation is without faith. The father clearly wants his son healed from his episodes of seizures but his lack of faith is the impediment to that happening. That is, until Jesus points it out to him. Faith is clearly the attribute or possession most needed out here for survival. Hebrews defines faith as the substance of things hoped for, the evidence of things not seen.

The usual context for the discussion of faith involves faith in Christ as a personal Savior, but I think faith takes on a new importance in scenarios like this deployment. I need faith everyday to generate the motivation to continue on the path before me, which involves getting up in a strange land and coming to the hospital and going through the same routine day in and day out without change. It is not unlike the routine of the popular movie "Groundhog Day."

The faith that sustains me is the one that allows me to take comfort in the fact that God is in control, even here in the middle of Iraq, and that I am here for a reason. I keep asking how long this will last, and I need sustaining faith to realize that when the time comes, we will come home under His care to reunite with our families.

This afternoon I had more time to look again at the pictures chronicling our lives together as parents that Ana sent. I can't think of anything else in my life that causes me so much satisfaction as being the father of Noah Michael, Logan Carson, and Caroline Maria. I know Ana will understand what I mean because even though our marriage brings satisfaction and is the foundation that makes parenthood possible, it does not produce the same feelings I get when I look at those pictures and see a living and breathing representation of me. The potential to miss six or eight or 10 months of their development may not seem like much when looking at the big picture of one's life, but it seems like an eternity to me right now.

Each day I try to strengthen my resolve to not return home and forget the things that I have learned while here. I pray that I never forget how blessed we are as a family, as a community, and as a nation. I have seen up close and personal the price that true freedom costs in terms of the loss of the lives of American soldiers, and it will stay with me forever. I pray that I will never forget that sacrifice and will never let my children or those around me forget that sacrifice.

24 Jun 03 – I'm caring for an 18-year-old male soldier who is psychotic. His psychosis is a new diagnosis and is really unusual in that he is almost catatonic or unresponsive to the outside world. He is not acting outwardly strange, but he won't do anything unless he is told. For instance, "Private, walk over there and sit on the bed. Now lie down." His unit reported to me that this behavior has been going on for several weeks, but they thought they could get him to snap out of it and didn't think much of it when he didn't because he wasn't harming himself or anyone else. The only effective way of treating him is to evacuate him out of theatre.

Our two nurse practitioners, who work in the Acute Care Clinic and do a lion's share of sick call each day, are having an open house in their area today that will include door prizes and snacks. Their flyers claim that they will award airline tickets to the US to the first ten attendees. This ploy is quite clever and is generating a considerable amount of buzz in the hospital. Whether they have real prizes or not, it is a great idea to raise the morale in the unit.

25 Jun 03 – A convoy arrived today with more mail. I experienced another Christmas-like event and received seven more packages – some that were mailed in early April and some that were mailed in early June. The highlights of this round of packages were breakfast items from Ana's parents, children's toys and clothes for distribution, pictures and cards from home and Logan's class at school, and the much awaited digital camera that Ana sent me in early April. While I have done well to copy photos from other cameras, I am happy to have one of my own. I am of the opinion that it is better to take too many pictures and sort them later than to come home with too few.

27 Jun 03 – I continue to trust and know that God has it all in His control, and I am just riding along to see where He is leading us. It is very easy to see the days marching by and feel frustrated that no obvious plan is emerging to have us come home. Today I

am taking today for what it is. Tomorrow will be another day closer to ultimately being home.

29 Jun 03 – We're treating a young Iraqi male that was involved in a crash and is still on respiratory and blood pressure support. He is essentially brain dead by our tests and assessment. His parents have been coming to visit and are openly upset about his condition. When they arrived today, we shared our finding with them and gave them our opinion that we should withdraw the artificial support from him. They were understanding and in agreement with our recommendation but pleaded with us to not do it today because they had no way of transporting him home to Kirkuk, and they did not have enough time to get him buried before sundown, as is their custom. All parties agreed that we would withdraw care in the morning and that would allow them adequate time to make the necessary arrangements. (He died within five minutes of us withdrawing the support).

Later in the afternoon yesterday I saw an interesting patient, one of the generals from the 4th ID who is a deputy commander for operations and intelligence for the division. He had been referred to see me for some non-specific symptoms he had been having over the past week. He was very personable and I enjoyed meeting him. Fortunately, I think he is just suffering from a virus, and I advised him to take it easy and have some of the labs repeated in several days. I told him that he should be fine.

30 Jun 03 – Rob D. went on another transfer to the Tikrit Teaching Hospital. All went well until he began to have a somewhat heated discussion with an older Iraqi physician who was hanging around on the periphery of the group. Rob said that he insisted on engaging him in a discussion about how the US was responsible for the problems in Iraq as a result of the embargos and so forth. Rob said that he allowed the man to speak his mind (fostering the concept of freedom of speech) until the man mentioned how Iraqis were benevolent and not harmful to other countries, at which point Rob said he bet the Kuwaitis would have a different opinion. The man immediately moved away.

01 Jul 03 – All across the United States today is the start of the

new academic year in most medical schools. It is the day that you transition from one class of medical school to the next and from one class of residency or fellowship to the next. For me, today started the countdown clock to when I will complete my service obligation to the Army for all my education. In another 364 days and a wake-up, I will separate from the Army and begin the next phase of my career in private practice. Right now I am not too choked up about that possibility, but I will allow for the fact that I'll probably be somewhat melancholy when the day arrives.

The preparations continue for the 4th of July picnic, and teams are being organized for volleyball, soccer, and football. Although not an official event, I noticed the appearance of a basketball goal on the pavement outside beside the DFAC tent this morning. When I came back from running, several soldiers were already playing a game of 3-on-3. Inside the DFAC new TV and satellite receivers were being installed.

We are struggling again to communicate with the Iraqis because the professor that was working for us last week has not been seen in four or five days. The 1st Medical Brigade states that they are busily working on hiring replacements, and in the meantime, we are playing a bizarre form of charades in a half-hearted attempt at communicating with the Iraqi patients. The issue of adequate numbers of translators should be highlighted as a huge issue in any after-action report concerning this war. I think we should employ Iraqi physicians until their health care system can get back on its feet. We are also still having trouble categorizing the Iraqis as civilian or EPW when they arrive because the circumstances of their injury are often sketchy.

04 Jul 03 – Happy 4th of July! Last night was unusually warm again, but at least there was a slight breeze.

At 0800 we held a ceremony to kick-off the festivities for the celebration. Several people spoke and read poems. Many shared letters received from back home that tried to capture the meaning of freedom and independence. We were all struck by the irony of celebrating freedom in a country that is not yet truly free. We also had prayer, sang patriotic songs, and posted the US flag to fly over our compound for the day. The first flag flown belongs to one of our nurse practitioners LTC Teresa H. It was from the funeral of her brother, an Air Force pilot who had given his life in an earlier conflict. Throughout the day, all others who had personal flags were allowed to raise them aloft and have a photo made and then bring them down again. My flag was the last one flown, and it flew until sunset.

There has been a volleyball tournament, a 3-on-3-basketball tournament, a chess tournament, a spades tournament, and a window decoration contest. I am proud to report that the ICU window that was built using the cards received from Logan's 1st grade class won second prize in the contest. The winning entry window was a fairly simple design that posted the names of all those soldiers who have given their lives to this point in this war.

06 Jul 03 – The 28th CSH-Tikrit admitted 80 patients in our first month of operation (8-30 Jun). The breakdown of patients was as follows: 29 patients to medicine, 18 patients to orthopedics, 21 patients to general surgery, and 13 patients to urology. Of those 80 patients, 57 were US soldiers. Thirty-five of the soldiers were treated and returned to duty, while the other 22 were evacuated out of here. The number of US soldiers injured in conflict was very small, while the injured Iraqis constituted the largest number of their admissions.

Bill is sending me the same data for Dogwood so that I can format my presentation slides the same way he has. I am sure that all the numbers will be much more impressive as Dogwood continues to be the busiest CSH in the entire theatre. They have had several periods of time over the past few days in which they were entirely at capacity and needed to scramble to discharge or transfer patients in order to be able to admit more. I continue to offer Bill the chance to come up here and catch a small break, but he prefers to stay put because he is established there. I can understand that feeling.

I received good news from Ana this morning via e-mail. It turns out that she sent a copy of our family 4th of July photo and e-mail greeting to the editor of the paper in Fayetteville, along with some details about our 4th of July family tradition to take a picture wearing

Old Navy summer t-shirts and how this year's picture came about. Since moving to North Carolina in 2000, Ana has had us take a yearly 4th of July photo in Old Navy flag t-shirts. This year, she created a split photo with a home shot of her and the kids next to a photo of me in uniform in Iraq with the same t-shirt on. She had mailed the shirt to me in enough time to ensure that the deployment did not spoil her yearly tradition. The editor liked the story so much that he decided to feature it in his opinion section of today's *Fayetteville Observer*. It really made my day to look at the online website and see our pictures there and read the words written about our family. I sometimes grumble when it comes time to take another picture with our family (mainly because it has historically been such a struggle trying to get three youngsters to cooperate) but now I am proud that my wife has insisted on establishing family traditions. I am also proud that his opinion piece will remind others at home that we are all still here and that our work should not be forgotten. I am proud of my wife for fighting the good fight at home. She, by far, has the hardest task at this point of the deployment in terms of keeping our children going and our household organized. She has my utmost respect.

07 Jul 03 – The temperature last night again was quite hot, and although the breeze should have felt good, it reminded me more of someone pointing a blow dryer at my face and leaving it set on low-warm. I eventually fell asleep and awoke to another warm morning.

After breakfast I joined COL G. for a planned visit to the Tikrit Teaching Hospital. There was a dual purpose to our trip; one of the soldiers needed an MRI of his wrist, and COL G. wanted us to attend the Grand Rounds that we had previously been invited to. None of the other providers felt they could attend today, so we also took along LTC Diane S., one of the nurse practitioners who staffs the Acute Care Clinic and does such a wonderful job.

Our convoy of two Humvees and an ambulance rolled through the streets of Tikrit without incident. The streets were more populated this morning than on my prior two visits into town. Not all stores appeared open, but the majority seemed to have activity.

Many of the merchants had their goods displayed on the sidewalk in front of their store. We saw predominately men, some women, but few children walking around on the streets and in the market place. We continue to hear and read that Tikrit is considered a hotbed of insurgent activity, but you would not suspect it from driving through the town. I should also mention that most of the attacks and hostile activity come after dark, and in that regard, maybe Tikrit is not so different from other cities the world over, where it is not wise to travel after dark anymore.

At the hospital, we were greeted warmly by the physicians and led into the conference room for the meeting. COL G. directed the soldier to the MRI suite and then joined the meeting. There were approximately 20 physicians and residents in attendance, both men and a few women. The Iraqi physician in charge asked if we had any interesting patients to present. When COL G. paused, I volunteered to discuss an Iraqi man with multiple electrolyte problems that I had admitted. Not knowing the format that they typically used, I nonetheless plowed forward by describing the patient's history and exam findings. Then I wrote his laboratory test values on the chalkboard and opened the discussion for questions and ideas from the other physicians. Several of them asked questions and offered helpful comments about the management. At the end of that discussion, there seemed to be another pause in the conversation.

Not wanting to allow the opportunity to get away to do some more teaching, I launched into a question and answer session concerning the management of atrial fibrillation, which is an irregular heart rhythm. When they realized I was a cardiologist, they quickly presented the case of a 15-year-old girl for my opinion. Because the conference was near completion, they asked if I would like to examine the patient, and we quickly moved upstairs to see her.

Following the physical exam, her attending physician suggested that we could repeat the heart ultrasound if I was willing. Again, I jumped at the request, and we moved downstairs to the radiology suite where they had an old, but functional, echocardiogram machine. With several providers hovering over my shoulder and the mother offering words of encouragement, I was able to determine that she did have a mass in her heart. I shared with them that I thought she would possibly need a surgical correction if the antibiotics couldn't clear the infection. However, I know in talking with the providers that there is no heart surgery being performed in Iraq just yet. They are hopeful that the services will become available again in Baghdad, but for now they must manage problems like this with medications.

Finishing our business there and having collected the soldier who came to have an MRI, we left that hospital and drove to the former military hospital that I had visited several weeks ago. On my first visit, there were not many physicians around. Today there were several, and they all welcomed us warmly. We were invited into the hospital director's office, which was actually quite nicely decorated and furnished by their standards. We sat in his office on one of the several sofas and talked with many of the providers on the staff. We were served hot tea in small demitasse size glasses while we talked. The tea was very sweet, just like a hot version of southern iced tea, and it suited my taste buds just fine. After a little while, we bid them farewell and returned in our convoy to Camp Speicher without incident.

08 Jul 03 – Flying in Army Blackhawk helicopters is fun! I say that because I had the opportunity to fly again this afternoon, taking a patient from here to Dogwood. The tasking fell to me because the surgeons were all tired from operating most of the night, and the ER guys were busy seeing patients. This was my second time transporting a patient during flight and my third trip overall on this deployment. It is an amazing feeling when the rotor revs up and we rise almost straight up in the air and then lean into a nice gradual banking maneuver away from the landing zone headed toward the destination. The in air portion is amazingly smooth, and you are just high enough to obtain a good visual perspective without being so high that you lose the detail.

Returning to Dogwood was interesting for me, and I was struck by how crowded it seemed there. The tent structure at Dogwood is more confining because the roof of the tent hangs lower than at Tikrit. The hospital at Dogwood requires the extra inner liner bag for chemical protection. The net effect is that someone of my height (~ 6 ft) needs to stoop over slightly to walk through certain sections of each tent. Returning caused me to remember that I used to spend much of my time here bent over.

The level of activity in the ER was also increased over that of Tikrit. Unfortunately, I was able to spend only a short time visiting there because the Blackhawk was standing by to return me to Tikrit. I went to the pharmacy to pick up some items to bring back and then, luckily, I was able to find Bill and spent a few minutes visiting with him. He said that things were basically proceeding as they had when I was there. He wished that I could stay longer, as did I, but it wasn't reasonable to keep the flight crew waiting. Our flight back was also uneventful but even more enjoyable because I did not have any patient care duties and could just stare out the window.

Iraq is a country of contradictions from the air. As I have mentioned before, Forward Logistics Base (FLB) Dogwood is located in the middle of a large sand trap, not far from the Euphrates River. Upon crossing the river, the landscape immediately changes from sand to lush vegetation. Flying along the outskirts of Baghdad, it is clear that there are affluent areas with large homes and manicured gardens, alternating with poorer slums. The landscape between Baghdad and Tikrit is a mixture of sandy regions with patches of scrub brush and then areas of lush greenery as the river passes by. The Euphrates River turns out of Baghdad and flows in a more northwesterly direction, while the Tigris River flows generally north. Along the Tigris River are the towns of Balad, Samara, and finally, Tikrit.

The other interesting feature I spotted from the air was the presence of portable irrigation systems that you see when you drive along fields in the more arid areas of the United States. These are tube systems that can be rolled around for positioning and have the tubes high in the air so the spray can come down like rain. The Iraqis have clearly been practicing irrigation in some areas because you can see green islands of growth in the midst of the sand.

09 Jul 03 – This afternoon I saw the general who I have been following over the past two weeks for what I thought was a viral ill-

ness. Today he reported feeling completely recovered, and his liver enzyme levels had normalized. He and I were both happy that he had recovered without any significant interventions, and we agreed that he'd wait and restart his cholesterol drug in three months to allow his liver to fully recover from its probable infection. In my limited experience, there seems to be a big difference between the general officers who are war-fighters and those who are politicians. This man was very genuine, and I enjoyed being his physician.

12 Jul 03 – The sunrise here is quite a striking sight. The flat terrain to the east allows you to see the sun emerge from below the horizon. The show lasts for over 20 minutes while the sphere with beautiful shades of red and orange is elevating into the sky. After 20 minutes it takes on the brighter yellow-orange color that prevents one from looking directly into it. I enjoyed this show for much of my run and made it back to the showers before almost everyone else.

13 Jul 03 – Today is Sunday, and Cal told me that today is day number 126 of the deployment. Eighteen Sundays ago we said good-bye to our families at Green Ramp and boarded the plane to bring us here. I cannot put into words how long ago that feels to me. When I look back through some of the pictures from those early days in Camp Doha and Camp Victory, it feels as if it were years ago. The images are still fairly clear, but the situations have changed so dramatically since then that I think my mind is telling me that certainly more time has elapsed.

14 Jul 03 – At approximately 0300 this morning we experienced a significant shift in our scope of practice when we received four injured children from an air-evac flight. They were all members of the same family that consisted of two boys, ages six and five, and two girls, ages four and three. The full details of the accident are unclear to us at this point, but we know the children were in a motor vehicle accident (MVA) and also sustained some shrapnel injuries. One fragmented version of the story said that the female driver of the vehicle (unknown relation) did not stop at a military checkpoint and was thus fired upon. The female was taken to an Iraqi hospital with unknown injuries.

The three-year-old girl was the most severely injured, having sustained a fracture of her skull and a brain injury. She was taken to the OR first for cleansing and debridement of this wound. She returned to the ICU in stable condition but with the potential for considerable brain swelling over the next few days. The next most seriously injured was the six-year-old boy, who sustained multiple shrapnel injuries to his chest and a single shrapnel injury to his head. He was very stable, but we were having real difficulty in localizing the exact position of the shrapnel in his brain and chest, given that we do not have a CT scan readily available. We evacuated these two children to Dogwood at around 0930 because they have the neurosurgeons and the CT scanner available.

The five-year-old boy sustained shrapnel injury to his left shoulder that required surgery, but he is doing fine post-operatively. The four-year-old girl escaped any serious injury and received only a small lump on her forehead. She slept most of the morning – all the children were very tired in the early morning hours and we had concerns that they had more serious neurological injuries that we were missing – but has been quite the charmer since she has been awake.

She has beautiful, thick black hair that falls around her shoulders and nicely highlights her friendly smile. We have not been able to identify any family members so far and will continue to nurture these two siblings until we do. The similarity in ages to my children has not been lost on me. I still feel uncomfortable seeing children in pain, but God props me up and allows me to focus on the tasks at hand while I am needed in the care giving process. Each day I attempt to create levity by wearing a humorous title on my shirt nametag. Most of the names have to do with cardiology or internal medicine such as "Director, Cardiac Cath Lab" or "Director, Tikrit Research Institute." Today I became, "Chief, Department of Pediatrics," which should give my pediatrician wife a pretty good chuckle.

15 Jul 03 – The highlight of my morning was finding a copy of the movie "Lilo and Stich" to show to the brother and sister who were in the ICU. I would say that they were as attentive as can be

expected given the fact that they don't understand the language. Like other children I have been around, they played on the floor while watching the movie on my computer, occasionally getting up and wandering away to play with a different person or toy before returning to watch.

We have had what seems like a non-stop stream of visitors from throughout the hospital to see these children. I had observed this reaction back at Dogwood also, and I think it speaks to most human beings' desires to care for children and make sure that they are all right. I don't think it is an attempt at any kind of propaganda campaign or quest. Rather, I think that most of us like to be around children, especially when they are hurt, and the lure is even stronger when the kids are cute.

By mid-afternoon we learned that the sister and brother we sent to Dogwood were doing well and were being returned to us. At the time of rounds, the helicopter arrived bringing them back, coinciding with a visit by the children's parents. Needless to say, it was a very happy and moving reunion as the relief on the faces of the parents and children was evident. Through our interpreter, we learned that the mother had been another woman in the vehicle but was not injured. Her brother did not survive, and we did not press for any more information at this point. We carefully explained the injuries of each child to them and answered their questions. The prognosis for all the children is very good.

17 Jul 03 – Today we built and occupied the physician's tent. We moved into it this morning and have slowly brought some things in that will establish it as our domain. Our half of the tent is the end where the ECU is installed, which is important because we receive the cool air first. In spite of us having the ECU on our end of the tent, the single ECU is not quite capable of cooling like the other tents in the hospital that are generally served by one ECU on each end. In this case, I think the chaplain, who shares the other end of the tent, will be the perfect advocate to pursue a second ECU on his end of the tent.

Late last night we received word that the 1st Med Bde intelligence was reporting that Camp Speicher was at risk of imminent attack from local insurgents, which prompted us to don our flack vests and helmets and assume defensive positions. For me, this entails reporting to the ICU, which is my area of responsibility during a MASCAL (mass casualty). After about an hour we were told that we could stand-down from the high alert, and most of us went to the LSA to go to sleep.

18 Jul 03 – Today was day two in our new physician's area, which we have yet to name. For now I think I'll call it the doctor's lounge. I managed to stay in the area pretty much all day, even though the mid-afternoon temperature became challenging to endure. The enlisted soldiers built a nice, large, conference-type table that sits in the middle of the room. Rob G. has built two other desk-type tables that sit along opposite walls, and we have pulled our camp chairs in to sit around the table. We also partitioned off the rear section to use as a sleeping area for naps or for call. In total, the space is coming together quite nicely, if we can just provide better cooling.

The morning and evening hours are quite pleasant, and most everyone has now learned where we are and comes here to find us for consultations or clinical questions. The size of the room is bigger, and the character is significantly different from "the flea bag" at Dogwood, but it is becoming a nice retreat. Late in the afternoon, we all convened around the computer screen to watch three episodes of M*A*S*H and realize how little things have changed since the Korean War in terms of combat health support.

As of today, the 30th Medical Brigade – which is now our unified command and control element – signed over control of the fixed facility in Baghdad named Ibn Sina to the 28th CSH to establish a level III hospital. The planning and conversion stages commence immediately. The proposed date for accepting patients in at least a limited manner is 16 August.

19 Jul 03 – It is later in the evening now, and Rob G.'s promotion party was quite a festive affair, complete with a good-natured roast, chips and salsa, cookies, and crunch and munch. Rob D. made the observation that the same snack foods show up at every celebration, and he looks forward to the day when we will have more variety again. Because Rob G. now calls Panama home, there was

Latin music for the celebration, and several of the more talented individuals were actually dancing a bit.

21 Jul 03 – Twelve years ago yesterday, Ana and I were married at the Plymouth Congregational Church in Coconut Grove, Florida, which is an area of Miami. We had known each other for two years, having met in the summer of 1989 in San Antonio at the Army Officer Basic Course. In a letter I received from her yesterday, she pointed out that she has been involved with me for more than one third of her life, and I have been involved with her for over one quarter of my life. We are in agreement that neither of us can really remember our lives before the other came along. Fourteen years is a long time to spend with someone, and we have forged a strong friendship and bond.

This deployment has stretched our limits of being able to rely upon one another by picking up the phone or just walking into the next room with a question. Ana has shouldered a tremendous amount of responsibility in keeping our household functioning and our kids prospering. By all accounts she and the children are doing well, and I continue to thank God for sustaining them in the same way He sustains me. I was able to talk to her briefly on the satellite phone and confirmed that she was having a good day and that she enjoyed the flowers that I had ordered for her before deploying. Borrowing another line from her, I missed her yesterday, but no more than I do on any given day. As she encouraged me in her letter, I will press on to finish the race that is before me and I will trust that God is working everything according to His perfect will (adapted from Acts 20:24).

23 Jul 03 – I just admitted a 30-year-old Iraqi male who is an EPW from a camp down near the main palace. He was brought in because of concern for his skin condition. He has, by far, the worst case of psoriasis that I've ever seen. He states that it was pretty well controlled until four weeks ago when he was incarcerated and stopped receiving his weekly medicine. His skin now is almost totally covered in raised plaques that are scaly. He has certain areas that also appear to be infected, at least superficially. The scaling skin is so extensive that it is difficult and painful for him to move, and his

arms and legs are bent into a position of comfort. Unfortunately, we have very little to offer him because we do not have any medicine for psoriasis except steroids, and they are not the first line drug. We are going to work on getting his classification relaxed a bit so as to be able to transfer to the Tikrit Teaching Hospital, where they may have more treatment options.

The biggest news of the day is the report of the death of Saddam's sons in Mosul, which is about 200 miles north of here. It is too early to ascertain what impact that news will have around here. There are many who think that the secret mission intensity is increasing and that the apprehension or elimination of Saddam himself is coming soon. We have heard several "experts" on the news speculate that Saddam is actually being hidden in Tikrit. I joked with someone today that I think I saw him in a field near the fence yesterday morning while I was running. I can't easily imagine what would happen if he were in Tikrit and was injured in some way in an attempted capture and was brought here to the CSH. Talk about having a story to tell your children and grandchildren.

25 Jul 03 – Yesterday I admitted a 40ish Iraqi female EPW – the first one that we have encountered – who had a noticeable facial droop and wasn't able to speak, making her diagnosis suspicious for a stroke. We were told that she was an EPW because she is a strong Ba'ath Party member. She claims to the interpreter that she was minding her own business in Kirkuk – northeast from here – when men came into her house and apprehended her. She has been somewhat reluctant to communicate with me, and in fact, hasn't spoken at all, preferring to write her answers, which is not inconsistent with a possible stroke. I am sending her tomorrow for a brain MRI to the Tikrit Teaching Hospital.

I spoke to Bill again this morning at Dogwood via the Army phone to catch up on any significant thing happening there. The biggest item of news with him was that Carol Y. arrived two days ago. Carol is a pulmonologist friend of mine from Ft. Bragg who has come to replace both Chris B. and Dave H. I talked briefly to Carol, and his major comments were about the heat and the sand. I can only imagine what a shock it is for him to be flown from North

Carolina and then from Kuwait City up to Dogwood. From the air, Dogwood looks about as depressing as you can imagine. It is not unlike a daytime lunar landscape because all you see for miles in any direction is sand.

The doctor's lounge has remained a little cooler today after Cal spent a considerable amount of time yesterday studying and modifying the air flow within and out of the plenum or hollow cloth tube that hangs from the ceiling of the tent and provides the cool air. Today while I was walking to the food line at 1630, the little thermometer on my belt loop read 110 degrees.

27 Jul 03 – Bill e-mailed me that he was going to Landstuhl, Germany, to accompany a soldier who has a serious pneumonia and is on the ventilator. While I am certainly jealous, I am happy that at least one of us is able to break away from this captivity for a little while. I am interested to see how long it will take him to return to Dogwood. I have confidence that Carol can certainly handle anything that happens there in his absence.

We are beginning to see more and more Iraqis with chronic medical problems end up in the EPW system, and when the unit medics are not able to care for them, they come here. I don't think this problem is going to easily go away.

This morning I discharged the 40-year-old female EPW back to custody after treating her low potassium. The longer she stayed with us, the more I became convinced she was making up a lot of her neurological symptoms. My suspicions were confirmed when her brain MRI done downtown yesterday came back absolutely normal, making it highly unlikely that she had suffered a stroke. More troubling was that she somehow made contact with her daughters while she was away from this hospital and was heard speaking to them by one of the attendants who accompanied her. For us, she had never spoken and only cried and wrote that she couldn't speak. This morning my patience and sympathy ran out, and she was released back to the camp.

Two days ago I was in the chapel listening to a live Internet radio broadcast from a rock station in John's hometown of Kansas City when he told me that he had written the DJ an e-mail and requested that she play a song for him and all the troops. After about 20 minutes of listening, she came on and dedicated a song to John K. and all the troops serving abroad. I was struck by how small the world has become with the evolution of the Internet and satellite technology.

29 Jul 03 – Yesterday evening we treated a 20-year-old soldier in the ER who was suffering from heat stroke and had a core temperature that had been measured at 108 degrees. This temperature is associated with a fairly high mortality rate. He had just arrived to his unit the day before yesterday and was spending his first full day in the heat of Iraq without the benefit of the air-conditioned tents he'd been accustomed to.

Miraculously, he seems to have sustained no damage to his brain, liver, or kidneys, in spite of the very high core temperature. The Lord certainly provided him with protection during a time when his extreme body temperature could have taken his life. By the Army regulations that govern policy about medical readiness, I am required to refer him to the medical evaluation board, which will decide if he may remain on active duty or be released because of the risk of this happening again. If he remains in the Army, he'll be restricted in the places he can be assigned. He will be evacuated out of theatre on the next transport.

Life around me appears to be progressing as usual. The temperature has not seemed quite as hot, but then again, it is all very relative because hot is still hot. Rob D. has suggested we call our physician's area "The Think Tank," and I agree it has potential. We'll float the idea by the other guys and see how it is received.

Bill wrote me from Landstuhl where he is having a nice break away from Dogwood. I received an e-mail from one of the ER nurses who recently left here to return to Dogwood. She said the mood is glum there because they are so busy, and the acuity of the injuries to US soldiers is very high. Everyone at both places is anxious to know what the future holds for each location and the fixed facility in Baghdad.

9 / August in Iraq

02 Aug 03 – Last night we admitted one of Saddam's former bodyguards. He came to us with a fractured elbow – that Rob G. is planning to repair surgically today – and an infection of his wrist that I am treating. He is also a diabetic but says that he doesn't take any medicines because he doesn't want to. He is not very imposing physically and so far has caused no problems. He seems to be like the other EPW's we have cared for, although he isn't talking as much. I can't help but wonder how many people this man has harmed.

I continue getting e-mails from Bill, who is still in Germany and planning to attend the German Grand Prix this weekend. I compiled our statistics again for our workload last month. In July we admitted 126 patients with 45 of the admissions being to my medicine service. The remaining patients were divided between the three surgeons.

04 Aug 03 – The past couple of days have been two of the hottest we have experienced while being here, and the overall morale is at a record low. Our commander has been telling us ever since we left the US that we should be prepared to remain here a year, even though none of us have really believed her. If that proves to be correct, all soldiers are eligible to take 14 days leave during months 5–10 of a long deployment. The catch in that policy is that no more than 10% of the total number of soldiers in a unit can be gone at any one time. That means that there are only 50% of the soldiers that are going to benefit from this policy, and I doubt that the physicians will even be considered because there is no one to cover for us when we go.

05 Aug 03 – Late this morning an American civilian contractor was driving his truck on a road near here and pulled off at one

of the roadside stands where they sell drinks, snacks, and ice. When pulling back onto the road, he apparently drove over the top of an explosive device, and it detonated underneath the cab of his truck. When he arrived here, he was not responsive and was blue in color from having lost most of his blood from serious explosion injuries to both lower legs. When placing bilateral chest tubes did not restore his heart rhythm, we decided to discontinue the chest compressions and drug resuscitation and pronounced him dead.

I do not know this man or the circumstances that brought him here, but I am angry right now with the residents of this country. We are not winning the hearts and minds of a small but significant number of Iraqi insurgents. The guerrilla warfare is very demoralizing to our troops and to us, the healthcare providers. Intellectually I realize that the vast majority of Iraqis are thankful for what we have done and for our presence. But the small, insurgent groups are beginning to make me want to just give this country back to them and go home and let them settle things in their own barbaric way. Of course, the proponents of the big picture view would say that we couldn't abandon Iraq until democracy is established because that will give the greatest assurance that they will not challenge the security interests of the United States. The problem with the big picture view is that we are the ones here on the ground either being attacked or having to deal with the attacks of the cowardly vermin that are having free reign here. The big picture is somewhat out of focus for us. We just want to go home, and that emotion is made all the stronger when we get the sense that no one wants us here.

Bill is still in Germany and is, appropriately, taking advantage of the time off. It is apparently fairly difficult to get back from there. I am told that this is because there are many soldiers traveling this way and that for someone who is traveling as a medical attendant – after having accompanied a patient there – the priority is very low, and they are routinely told to check back in two to three days or even more. It is evident that if you get there and want to "disappear" for a few days, there is ample opportunity.

I am really struggling with my emotions toward the former bodyguard. I don't think I have ever been forced to care for someone as a patient who was a known criminal that is probably guilty of numerous incidents of unspeakable evil and brutality. For the most part, as a medical staff, I don't detect that we have any particular prejudice against the Iraqi prisoners. We often joke with them on rounds, and I believe that we treat them with the same courtesy and respect that we afford the Iraqis who are not prisoners. They almost always make this possible because they appear truly remorseful for what they have done. I can only recall one patient at this facility in Tikrit that has maintained an aggressive attitude while he was here. Our response to his aggression was to blindfold him the majority of his time here. There have been many others whose expression was very hard on admission, and we thought that they were "bad" guys, only to have them soften significantly over time and become just as personable toward us as all the rest.

This bodyguard has a hardened face some of the time, but he is also quick to be appreciative when we make bedside rounds and inquire how he's feeling and offer him pain medicine when he needs it. Yesterday we showed him his picture in the Stars and Stripes that showed him blindfolded immediately after his capture. We tried to joke with him about it, but he was not in a joking mood. In retrospect, I can understand why. I'd like to say that I took some sort of pleasure in kidding him, but down deep it made me uncomfortable. I guess that there is something that rings true about the Biblical principle of repaying your enemy with kindness because in doing so, it will have the effect of heaping burning coals on his head. I am not so optimistic as to expect to see a visible change of heart on his part, but his presence has caused me to deal with new feelings, and that is always a good thing in the maturation process.

07 Aug 03 – Earlier this afternoon, another convoy was attacked less than 5 miles from the front gate of Camp Speicher, injuring one soldier who was then brought here for care. Fortunately, he only sustained a fracture to his leg caused by shrapnel from the homemade bomb that was detonated as they drove by. I spoke with another soldier who was riding in the same vehicle. He said they were riding along the main highway between Baghdad, Tikrit, and Mosul. Without warning, he heard a loud explo-

sion before the driver was hit and pulled the vehicle to the side of the road. After assessing their injuries, they flagged down another convoy that assisted them and brought them here.

09 Aug 03 – The temperature has continued to climb here each day, and late yesterday afternoon our ability to remain reasonably cool inside the hospital came to an abrupt halt as first one, then two, and finally, all three of our power generators went offline. I am told that for two of them, the problem was that they overheated and had a malfunction in the radiator cooling system. The cause of failure in the third one was apparently a head gasket. Initially, it was only one generator, and that meant that the power grid had to be rearranged, but most of the vital areas continued to function. It didn't take long, however, for the second generator to succumb to the increased workload caused in taking on the work of the first generator. Once the second generator stopped, we became mission incapable because the OR was no longer functional on only one generator.

At that point we began to open the windows on the tents, looking for any slight breeze to blow in. When the third generator came down, the indoor temperatures became virtually unbearable. While a team of soldiers went to look for another generator to borrow from someone on post, we began to consider the possibility of moving our patients to somewhere that still had air-conditioning. While all this was going on, I went outside to use the latrine, and my pocket thermometer was pegged at 120 degrees, and there was absolutely no breeze around. We all went and changed into our PT uniforms and began using all the cooling devices we could find, including hand-held fans, portable misters, cold towels, and such. The only thing in our favor was that it was around 1800 by the time it happened, and the sun was beginning its drop from the sky. The breeze thankfully picked up somewhat, and we struggled on for about 90 minutes before the maintenance guys got the first, then second generators back on line. This allowed us to power up the essential areas like the OR, EMT, ICU, and ICW, and make the patients more comfortable again.

The maintenance section receives big kudos for their role in this crisis, as they were effective at getting most things back on line quickly. They continued to work until 0130 this morning to repair the third generator. The mission to find another generator was successful, and we now have one in reserve plus one to scavenge parts from should they be needed. At present, the maintenance staff is working to cover the generators with camouflage netting to reduce some of the radiant heat. I am praying that their measures will be enough because the temperature today was forecasted to exceed the temperature yesterday. I am not looking forward to a repeat performance.

I can say with confidence that this latest wrinkle has added another dimension of loathing of this place. In these past few days, I have been the hottest that I have ever been, and I am not very encouraged by it all. I am thankful that the Lord has protected me and the other members of the hospital from becoming heat casualties. It is amazing to me when I drink fairly consistently all day long and expect to go outside to the latrine and never do. Not to belabor my potty habits too much, but I used the latrine this morning after the run and then again late this afternoon. Of course, I realize that the best approach is to just keep cool and keep drinking, both of which have become my primary objectives at this point. Once again, life on a deployment has been broken down to very simple terms.

12 Aug 03 – It has been several days since I have written, and it is all because of the temperature tribulations we have been going through. For one thing, our physician's area – the Think Tank – is now only cooled between the hours of 2100 and 0900 in order to reduce the ECU use in non-clinical areas. The second reason is that I have been too busy and haven't had the desire to sit and write. Most spare minutes in the past 48 hours have been used to catch my breath or catch a catnap or both. I am maintaining a fairly even keel – only by the pure, abounding grace of God – and am being careful not to become a heat casualty myself.

The temperature has remained beyond miserable. I cannot think of enough words to describe how hot it is. In addition, there is very little change in the temperature between day and night. The night-shift workers are finding it almost impossible to sleep during the day because the designated sleep tent has been turned off to save power, and the dayshift workers can't sleep that well at night because the temperatures are barely dropping below 100 degrees. Due to the recent patient acuity, I have been sleeping in the hospital for the past two nights and getting some relief that way, although with frequent interruptions for patient care issues. I don't think the sweating stops from about 0800 until around 2300 each night, and my decrease in urination is correlating well with the rising temperatures.

Three days ago we experienced generator problems at 1600, the next day at 1400, and yesterday the generator failures began at 0930. That was also the same time that the heat casualties began to be brought in. I think we have admitted around 15–20 patients for heat injury over the past few days. Most of them have been US soldiers and a few Iraqi civilians and EPW's. Some of them have had true heat stroke with mental status changes that required intubation and rapid evacuation. One of the major challenges we faced yesterday was trying to cool these patients down when our ambient temperature in the hospital was between 105–110 degrees in some areas and over 115 degrees in other areas. At one point in the mid-afternoon, there were six soldiers brought in simultaneously to the ER for heat illness, and the ER temperature was 108 degrees. One of the principles of managing heat injury is to cool the outer body, but the recent temperatures inside our tents are making that almost impossible.

Yesterday afternoon I admitted an EPW for heat stroke that was also thought to have a heart condition. He was intubated and sedated but was noted to have changes on his EKG consistent with cardiac ischemia. Later in the day, his cardiac enzymes showed that he had actually had a heart attack. My management of his heart attack has been complicated by the fact that he also appears to have a gastrointestinal bleed that prevents me from giving him blood thinners to prevent any further clots from forming in his arteries.

Late last night another EPW was admitted with heat stroke that was also complicated by a seizure and respiratory arrest. My initial treatments for him led to him dropping his blood pressure and needing to have strong medicines started to raise the pressure again. They are both very seriously ill, and neither is showing any signs of significant brain activity. My plan will be to sedate them for the first 24–48 hours and then try to wake them up to see if their cognitive function returns.

I cannot help but awaken each day and dread the rising of the sun because I know that there is nothing but hardship ahead. It seems that each challenge pushes us farther and farther to our limits of tolerance. When we first arrived in country, it was the newness of the area and the threat of imminent war and then the SCUD attacks. Then we experienced the arduous convoy and the fear of traveling without any reasonable security measures. Next it was the omnipresent sand and windstorms at the Dogwood location. Now it is the oppressive heat and physical strain that comes with working for weeks on end without a day off or break. And throughout the deployment, we have existed in conditions that would be considered sub-human by most people's standards if the truth were known. In sum total, it has probably been the most concentrated difficult experience I have ever lived through.

My morning devotional from the Our Daily Bread series was taken from the 4th chapter of Philippians, and I think the Lord was truly exhorting me today to "rejoice in all things, and again, rejoice." Rejoicing in the midst of this deployment is not often the first choice that comes to my mind, but I am pressing on and striving to do just that. It is a one-day at a time, gradual process.

August is classically the hottest month of the year in Iraq, and then things cool down as September arrives. An old Iraqi saying has been repeated several times around here in the past few days that says, "The first 10 days of August are hot enough to melt the hinges or handles off the door, the second 10 days will dry and consume the remaining fruit, and the third ten days will usher in the winter. As of today, I guess we have eight more days to go. We were offered some relief today because the winds were gusting throughout the day – almost to shamal-type strength – and that served to circulate the air better through the generators, and we didn't experience a single power failure. Through various acquisition methods we now have enough generators to add a fourth one to the grid and thus reduce the load to each individual generator and still have one to two in reserve.

One Iraqi patient we have now has sparked a philosophical, ethical and legal debate. He is on a hunger strike because he wants to die in captivity. We have debated the ramifications of giving him intravenous nutrition and fluids against his will. We all concluded that we didn't know the answer and should probably address the question to the legal folks for advice and guidance.

13 Aug 03 – After several days of heat that defied all logic, the temperature dropped last night and made sleeping once again bearable. In fact, it was so pleasant that this morning I was actually chilly when I awoke before dawn and had to crawl into my sleeping bag, which is something I hadn't done in weeks. The cooler weather continued through the day today – at least in relative terms. I think the high was still around 117 degrees, but it was amazing how much cooler that felt. We were able to leave the air-conditioning running in our Think Tank until around 1300 today before needing to flee from the heat. I think God again realized the limits we had reached in the past few days and spared us having to face the challenges today.

Instead, we were faced this morning with the challenge of another soldier dying. Shortly after 0700 we heard over the radio net that a medevac flight was inbound with a seriously wounded soldier with a partial limb amputation. The soldier's condition was far more severe than described and he arrived blue with chest compressions being done. Cal immediately opened his chest with a scalpel and began open heart massage with his hand. Cal found that his heart was not beating and was empty, the cause of which was obvious if you looked at his legs. He had been the driver of an armored vehicle that had run over an explosive device that had basically blown his right foot off and severely mangled his left leg all the way up to the hip. On close inspection, all the wounds of his leg were clotted, which suggested that he had lost all his blood. The medevac crew reported that they had performed CPR on him for over 20 minutes before arriving to us. At that point, we realized that our efforts were futile and the resuscitation was halted.

At the conclusion of the resuscitation effort, I heard many of the EMT staff talking about their ongoing concerns over why we are here. I observed pure despair in many of their faces, but to their credit, they were moving about, cleaning up, and preparing for the next emergency that is bound to come. Our Iraqi interpreter was also visibly shaken by this death, and I heard him tell someone that his people are so unaccustomed to the concept of freedom that they think it can only be obtained by killing. Naturally, this incident triggered an internal assessment in me concerning my attitude about our presence here. Today my attitude was more positive than on other days, and I didn't feel myself ranting about the injustices as much as I have on other occasions.

Today the Lord impressed upon my heart that there was much work yet to be done here, and He reminded me of all the soldiers we had saved by our existence here. I don't want to stay here another minute longer from this point, but I also realize my sanity depends upon trying to keep the bigger picture in focus. Our interpreter continues to remind us that if we weren't here, there would be rivers of blood from the internal battles between the various factions. I think he realizes that we are all fatigued and dwindling.

14 Aug 03 – We learned late in the day yesterday that Cal would be leaving this morning to return to Dogwood. He is to be replaced by John L., who is a general surgeon that had accompanied us originally to Tikrit but then had been pulled back to Dogwood on the first day here to cover for another surgeon who had gone to Germany. As I have mentioned, Cal has wanted to return to Dogwood for some time because he feels that it is one step closer to being replaced or at least getting assigned to accompany a patient to Germany. After Cal had finished packing last night, I joined him and the two Robs for a last night of cigars and reminiscence. We all agreed that the time here has been well spent, and we were able to specifically name the patients that have benefited from our care. We also charged Cal with being the new advocate for implementing the physician rotation policy that would bring new doctors here

to replace us. At the very least, he will be able to give us a firsthand accounting of the situation at Dogwood and the proposed move to the new hospital at Ibn Sina.

The evening temperature was very pleasant again, and the full moon added another element to our time spent together. The temperature continued to fall through the night, and we again awoke to a cool morning requiring sleeping bags or covers. The morning rounds were rapidly conducted, and we then gathered on the flight tarmac as the helicopter arrived from Dogwood to deposit John, an ICU nurse, and an Iraqi child that was being transferred here for further testing. As John disembarked and Cal prepared to get onboard, there were hugs and handshakes all around. It was good to see John, and he seemed genuinely pleased to arrive.

The patient being transferred is a 16-month-old Iraqi boy who was admitted at Dogwood about a week ago from an outlying medical clinic for fever and vomiting. In taking the history, it became evident that the little boy was developmentally delayed and very small for his age. The neurology team at Dogwood had done their evaluations to completion but felt the patient should have a head MRI performed to rule out a structural brain abnormality. At present time, the MRI at the Tikrit Teaching Hospital is the only one available to the 28th CSH either here or at Dogwood, so the plans were made to send the boy here for us to coordinate the study. In addition, we have been told that there is a pediatric neurologist assigned to the 4th ID somewhere in this area. The connection there is interesting because he was a senior resident in Pediatrics at WBAMC in El Paso when Ana started there in 1992, and we haven't seen or heard from him in 10 years.

The boy's father accompanied him and said that he had a relatively normal birth in an Iraqi hospital and seemed like his older sister and brother in development until about the age of 6–8 months, when they noticed that he wasn't sitting up or rolling and didn't reach as much for things like he had before. He was seen by an Iraqi general physician in January of this year and was diagnosed with a neurological condition and given folic acid to take each day. Since being at Dogwood, the records reflect that he has gained about 1 kg (2 lbs) in weight and eats fairly well. He has occasional choking and coughing following a meal. He has no episodes of turning blue or breathing problems.

16 Aug 03 – One of the Iraqi patients with heat injury has had his breathing tube removed and is doing fine, although I have some concerns about his mental status not being fully recovered. He sustained a fairly moderate-sized heart attack during his resuscitation and will now begin cardiac rehabilitation to the best of our ability to do it. I am petitioning for him to be re-classified from EPW status, but that decision is way outside my lane.

The second patient has not awakened and remains on the ventilator. In fact, both yesterday and today I formally assessed his brain function and found that he is in a persistent vegetative state, or coma. He also sustained a heart attack, although a much smaller one, and I am recommending we have him re-classified as well. The next step clinically is to place a tracheotomy in his throat for long-term breathing and a feeding tube for nutrition.

18 Aug 03 – It is Monday morning, and I am going to catch up with the events of the past two days. Two nights ago we received word that Dogwood had received several – between 18 and 24 – casualties from an EPW prison that had been attacked by mortar fire. The details are still under investigation, but there were several surgeries that arose that night from that attack, and when I spoke to Bill this morning on the phone, he said that most of the patients they received were still at Dogwood. He mentioned that they had received the Reuter's cameraman that had been shot yesterday but didn't survive. Bill also told me that the move to Baghdad is beginning in the next day or so, with doctors and patients going in batches. It should be completed by the end of this week, and Bill and Carol Y. were going to be on the last trip. He also said that Dogwood has around 55 patients and the majority are Iraqis who were all going to be moved.

Last week there were rumors that we were being considered to receive small containers not unlike our milvans to sleep in. We had seen these small trailers down at Camp Doha back in March and thought they looked fairly desirable. This week it seems the rumors are closer to becoming reality. There was a survey team here measuring our LSA and deciding how many of the trailers we would need. They are reported to have air-conditioning but apparently are very small, and it is rumored that we will be allowed a living space of 8 x 7 feet.

I attended church services yesterday and was pleasantly surprised to see Steve B. there, who attends church with me back in Fayetteville. He is the XO (Executive Officer) of an aviation unit nearby and though he had stopped by on other occasions to check on his soldiers, yesterday was the first time he'd come to church.

The Iraqi child is unchanged and went to the teaching hospital this morning to have his head CT performed. The pediatric neurologist came yesterday and evaluated the child and returned again today to review the results of the study. His suspicions about diagnosis were confirmed when the CT scan showed poor myelination of a large area of the brain tissue. Myelin is a component of nerve cells that is similar to the insulation on electrical wires and is responsible for speeding up the nerve transmission rate. Based on the child's history and exam findings, it is clear that he has some sort of non-myelination disease of his nervous system that results in the poor muscle tone and has also produced blindness that was confirmed with examination of his eyes.

This is a problem of metabolism that has been present since birth but only began to manifest as he grew older and did not reach his developmental milestones like he should. Unfortunately, there is no cure, and the muscle weakness will likely result in him being overwhelmed by a respiratory infection at some point in the future.

19 Aug 03 – This morning the field sanitation team closed off the burnout latrines and officially opened the porta-potties for business. I hope the contract for keeping them drained has been solidly established. If not, there are still plenty of deserts around us, and I am now skilled at cat-hole hygiene from my days on the convoy and the early days of being at Dogwood. The fourth generator was added today to the power grid, and everything seemed to proceed smoothly.

Recently a representative of COL Gagliano from the 30th Med

Bde asked Bill and me, to present a medical lecture to a group of Iraqi and Army physicians in Baghdad. The 30th Med Bde is forming a joint medical society and Bill and I have tentatively agreed to present the lecture if the transportation details can be arranged.

As I was coming back to the Think Tank at dinnertime, I saw the breaking news report that an explosion had damaged the UN building. At this point we don't know about the number of casualties, but it is not out of the question for us to receive some patients if the resources of Dogwood and the 21st CSH at Balad are overwhelmed.

21 Aug 03 – My older Iraqi patients are status quo, and we learned that it may be quite easy to have them reclassified as civilians. The Provost Marshall is supposed to be sending some documentation over in the next few days that would do just that. John L. successfully gave the one patient a feeding tube and tracheotomy today, while the other patient continues to get stronger on his own. I would be able to move them at any time we have acceptance from an Iraqi physician at one of the two hospitals we've visited.

We never received any casualties from the bombing of the UN building in Baghdad, but we watched parts of the coverage just like everyone else. I was struck by one editorial that I read online yesterday that proposed the idea that this event would cause President Bush to rethink his involvement of the UN in the rebuilding of Iraq. I will be interested to see if that is the effect of the bombing or if we'll just bring more troops back in to establish better order. Yesterday afternoon there was an ambush near the market area in Tikrit off a street that is locally referred to as "RPG Alley." The two injured soldiers brought here were members of a Special Forces unit. By the account I heard, they were in the market area to make some purchases when an Iraqi vehicle appeared out of nowhere and began firing. The two soldiers suffered lower extremity wounds, and an Iraqi interpreter with them was killed. I also was told that there were several Iraqi deaths, but those victims were not brought here. As has been the habit for US soldiers lately, we arranged for air-evacuation last night, and the helicopters arrived around 2300 for the trip to Kirkuk, where they would be met by a CCAT team for the transfer to Germany.

This afternoon we received some Georgian soldiers who had been burned while trying to dispose of a weapons cache. They were combat engineers who apparently allowed themselves to be too close to the pile of ordnance and it flared up in a flash. We think we'll be able to evacuate them out of theatre just like we would if they were US soldiers. Fortunately, one of the medics in the ER named SPC Z. speaks Russian and has been invaluable as an interpreter. The ones who are able to speak have been effusive in their thanks for the care they have received. Simple gratitude, when sincere, is worth more than any amount of riches, especially in an environment like this.

23 Aug 03 – I have just returned from a morning convoy in which we transferred the two Iraqi patients to the former military hospital. They were both unchanged in their condition over the past few days; the one in a coma and the other was recovering from his heart attack. Two days ago we had received the documentation that reclassified them as civilians and made the arrangements to transfer them. The Iraqi physicians were hospitable as always and thanked us for the care we had provided the men. I felt the gratitude was deserved in the man who was recovering from the heart attack, but I felt somewhat embarrassed to receive praise for the other patient because it is unlikely that he'll ever awaken. I am not sure we performed any great service by reviving him when he came into the ER in respiratory arrest, but those are not decisions that we are allowed to make going into the scenario, even in the US.

After getting the patients settled in safely, we were escorted back to the medical director's office where we were served hot, sweet tea in small glass demitasse-style cups. This was my second visit to this physician's office, and it was the second time I had been served in this fashion. I believe it is reflective of what the normal social activity would dictate. In situations like this, I always find myself wishing that all the Iraqis would meet us on the same level that the physicians do because we could then avoid the bloodshed and strife. The director's office was nicely furnished by the Iraqi standards that I have seen and contained several sofas, chairs, and a large cabinet TV with satellite reception. They pointed out to me that satellite TV was a new experience for the majority of Iraqis because the former government had prohibited it. One of the physicians remarked that much of their impression of the US would be influenced in the future by what they see on TV. This thought did little to reassure me.

Before arriving at the hospital, we had dropped off the child with the neurological illness and his father at a bus station where they planned to catch a bus to carry them back to their home in Baghdad. He was appreciative for all the help that we had provided in caring for his son and introducing the pediatric neurologist who had given him the unfortunate but true news about his son's disease and prognosis. Several of us took an unofficial money collection for the father and gave it to him prior to them leaving. We were touched by his obvious love for his son and his dedication that included selling their home and quitting his job as a building contractor to try to find the cause for his son's illness. I can only speculate what will become of them at this point, but I think that we collectively provided a service in being able to define the problem and help them achieve some closure on the issues.

I will admit that I was not as anxious to be on the convoy today as I had in the past. Usually I enjoy getting out and having a change of scenery, but with all the recent attacks on other convoys, I was more than a bit nervous until we pulled safely back onto Camp Speicher. I think the change of scenery and the interaction with the Iraqi physicians was helpful for my mood, and I feel better than I did this morning. We could really do a great deal of good for this country if they would only allow us. The physicians seem to always soak up any current knowledge that I pass along in our conversations, and the patients we care for seem to understand our intentions. My prayer is that they will continue to spread that message to their family and friends, and before we leave we'll be able to travel to the hospitals safely without fear of being attacked.

24 Aug 03 – It's Sunday morning here, and I have just attended our weekly service. As I write this, I realize that the message couldn't have arrived at a better time for me. Actually, it wasn't the scheduled message but one given by Steve B. during a time of testimony that spoke to me the most today. I have mentioned Steve before as a member of my church back home. During the testimonial time

prior to our morning prayer, Steve stood and encouraged everyone to not lose sight of the spiritual big picture, that is, to keep in mind that our being here is within the perfect will of God. We should avoid missing the blessings that He intends for us because we are so focused on the hardships. He was speaking about his own attitudes, but it certainly applied to all of us, especially me because I realize that the hardships have been *the* focus of my mind lately. I dwell on the heat and the dust. And I think about the unfairness of being away from my family and friends, while I lament the lack of comfort.

Steve's comments were meaningful for me because I certainly haven't stopped lately to consider my blessings. When I do that, I realize that in spite of my hardships, I have been doing well. I have plenty to eat and drink, and my workplace is air-conditioned. My cot is comfortable enough that I am getting sleep each night, and my health has been strong thus far. But most important is that I am being given the opportunity to grow closer to God through our struggles. Now I need to channel my desire to grow from this experience into a mindset that can carry me on a daily basis. I know that is what my daily Scripture reading and prayer time is supposed to accomplish, but it is good to have reminders like today to help me re-focus.

We instituted our new policy this morning of not having our usual 0730 rounds as a group on Sundays but instead round on our patients independently. This change gives us a chance to "sleep in" a little or at least not be rushed to gather information before coming to group rounds. It also allows us to take more time to enjoy breakfast or maybe watch the world news on the TV. I took advantage and lounged in my cot until well after sunrise and then enjoyed pancakes and hash browns at the DFAC. All the other physicians also seemed to enjoy the new approach, and we decided to make it a permanent change to our habits.

There is a team of physicians and investigators here from Washington to gather information about the cases of soldiers with pneumonia that have received so much press attention lately. I am scheduled to spend some time talking with them later this afternoon. For now they are reviewing our patient charts.

25 Aug 03 – Just after noon, a medevac chopper arrived with a patient that was supposed to be a soldier with a partial amputation of his hand. When they arrived, it was an Iraqi who had a partial amputation of his right hand but also had a complete amputation of his left hand and was also burned over 90% of his body. Apparently he was injured while trying to carry off some artillery shells because of the copper they contained, but they went off, causing the blast injury and subsequent fire. He is now in the ICU but has very low blood pressure, and his chances of survival are nearly zero. Our chaplain, John K., and Salam, our interpreter, have already prayed over him both in English and Arabic and administered the Muslim version of last rites.

28 Aug 03 – Just as Rob D. and I were planning a quick trip to the PX, we heard that there were helicopters landing with several wounded soldiers on them requiring urgent attention. When the choppers arrived, they brought five wounded Special Forces soldiers whose two-vehicle convoy had been ambushed between here and Kirkuk. Each of the physicians took a patient, and I was made responsible for the driver of vehicle number two, a 26-year-old sergeant who was a communications specialist. He told me that he noticed an Iraqi vehicle speed ahead of them and pull in line in front of the lead convoy vehicle and then slow down. This maneuver allowed the trailing Iraqi pickup to open fire into the American vehicles. He stated that he lost control of the civilian SUV he was driving, and it rolled down a short embankment, ejecting one of the rear seat passengers.

The wounded were triaged to surgery, waiting, or immediate evacuation to Baghdad. For now, there are several Special Forces soldiers milling around in the hospital while they await word on their buddies. This is the same group that contained the soldiers injured about 10 days ago when they were attacked in the Tikrit market area.

Yesterday I admitted an Iraqi EPW who is a type – I diabetic who was here a few weeks ago. He has reported himself as being a distant cousin of Saddam Hussein and was brought to our ER yesterday with mental status changes and rapid breathing that was being caused by a lack of insulin. When we were able to stabilize him, he reported that he had been without insulin for almost two days and had been getting no response from his pleas to the guards. By early this morning, his sugar levels and electrolytes had returned to almost normal. My big challenge now is finding out how to prevent this from happening again because this is his second admission for the same problem with this event being worse than the first. I'd like to consider getting his status re-evaluated like we'd done with the other two EPW's, but I think this guy is actually a bad guy, and we probably don't want him running around out there. He is young – 32 – and could likely give the US forces some real problems, especially if he's loyal to his cousin.

I finally talked to Bill down at Baghdad yesterday for about 20 minutes. He said the move had taken place in a fairly tolerable fashion and that they were getting settled into the new hospital. He says that it is very nice compared to anything we've encountered so far in Iraq as the 28th CSH. He described the patients being in rooms on the second and third floors with three sets of rooms on the ends of the hallways being designated for the ICU patients. He also said that their sleep area was nice and had air-conditioning and a sink in each room. He is sharing a room with Carol Y. and Jerome P., and on their floor there are three common area bathrooms with showers that he says are usually open. The only drawback at the moment is they are still suffering from inadequate power supply and must turn the power off in the sleep areas from 0800 to 2000 each day. Working in the hospital, he says, is just like being in an older, community-type hospital back home. There are 78 beds total with 21 of those being for ICU patients. They have the ability to run five OR tables if needed. Overall, the pace there is reasonable, and he says morale has significantly improved.

Trying to take advantage of a little-known paternity leave policy, he is applying to spend two weeks at home to see John Henry, who was born in April. I am fully supportive of him doing this and will be upset if the command doesn't work this out in his favor. I'm sure

Carol Y. can handle the Internal Medicine and Critical Care needs for a while to let Bill get away. I have now started to think again about going down there to switch places with Carol for a week or two when Bill returns because I'd like to see the facility, and it'd be a good change of scenery for me.

01 Sep 03 – Today is Labor Day. We are in the midst of a celebration of sorts, or at least as close as one can get while on a deployment in Iraq. Since Saturday there has been ongoing volleyball and basketball tournaments. The volleyball is in the sand, obviously, and the basketball is being played on a makeshift full-court that is set up out by the DFAC on the concrete. The volleyball tournament is made up of only teams from our unit, while the basketball is an invitational format that has attracted quite the crowds over the past two evenings. Today there are competitions for chess and spades players. My involvement has been that of an observer.

For the first time, I allowed myself to consider that the commander may be right about the year long deployment and what the implications would be if we did not redeploy until next spring – February or March. I don't like to consider not being with my family for Thanksgiving, my birthday, Christmas, and New Years. During worship yesterday, we mentioned the topic of being away from our families for Christmas, and it was a difficult image to think about. Several members of our "church" have mentioned it several times in the recent weeks, but I have blocked it out of my mind. Now I am being forced to face it as a possibility, as we are almost at the six-month mark, and there is no effort being made on any level to redeploy us anytime soon. If we are here at Christmas, I will only survive with the help of God above and the help of my Christian friends who are here.

On a much brighter note, I was able to talk on the phone to Ana and the kids early this morning. I got up at 0400 here and placed the call using the Army phone to connect to a worldwide operator, who connected me to an operator at Ft Bragg, who dialed my calling card number. I lost the connection at various stages twice before finally completing the call. The link was decent, and we were able to talk for 40 minutes. It was the first time I'd spoken to them in about

2 months, and it was sorely needed. The kids all seemed excited to talk to me. Noah caused me sadness because he told me he really missed me, and I know he understands what is happening and truly feels it. I miss them all so badly that it hurts. I especially worry that I am absent for too much in their development. I also miss my best friend, Ana. We have been communicating more lately with instant messaging on the Internet, but it's never the same as hearing the voice.

As it stands now, Bill and I are scheduled to give our lectures for the continuing education conference sponsored by the 30th Med Bde in Baghdad on Wednesday 10 September. I'd like to arrange for Carol to come here when I go there, if we can work that out. His only real concern is that it might be easy getting me there and him here, but the constraints on transportation put us in jeopardy of not making the switch back when the time comes. It is my intention to iron out the details over the next few days and make the switch next week when I get the chance.

03 Sep 03 – We had an ironic injury occur last night. A female soldier from another unit was visiting the palace compound taking advantage of the MWR (Morale, Welfare and Recreation) offerings that have been established by the 4th ID for their soldiers. She had just finished playing a game of volleyball and was walking toward the showers when she felt a sharp pain in her lower left leg. She looked down and saw that she was bleeding. It turns out that she had been wounded by an AK-47 bullet that was likely at the end of its travel trajectory because it broke the skin and bounced into her leg, but did not fracture it. She was successfully operated on last night and will now evac for rehabilitation.

Morale in this unit was intentionally lowered another notch today when COL G. began to enforce the recently emphasized theatre policy that all soldiers – without exception – should be in their uniform tops at all times. We have basically ignored this policy within the hospital because it doesn't make sense to wear your uniform top when it is likely that it will be soiled with blood and body fluids. However, during a recent visit, the 30th Med Bde sergeant major made a big deal of the fact that we were all violating a theatre policy. I guess the 30th Med Bde doesn't have enough "important" things to think about like how can we improve the supply system or how can we optimize the medical assets or, better yet, what the end-state combat health support plan is for this theatre. As far as I'm concerned, these things take far higher precedence than what uniform policies we are violating while we provide tip of the spear healthcare to US soldiers. I am very angry about this latest "clarification" of policy, and it has the effect of making me even more bitter about the lack of true common sense leadership that I have seen on this deployment.

05 Sep 03 – I spent the morning compiling the end of month reports for August. We had 152 admissions – our most to date – which was up from 126 in July. Of those 152 admissions, I had roughly a third, and the three surgeons split the other two-thirds fairly evenly. After finishing this task, I then switched to working on the upcoming lecture on heart failure that I am scheduled to give in Baghdad next week. I had written a lecture on this topic several years ago, and could have given that version, but there have been several updates in our treatment of this illness. This has been a good opportunity to update my talk. My preparation is going well, and I look forward to going down there, although I still don't know many details about the intended audience. For instance, I don't know if there are to be any Iraqi physicians or if it will only be the staff from Ibn Sina.

07 Sep 03 – It is Sunday here, and another week has passed by in our deployment. The morning worship service was inspirational, and we took part in a communion service, as we do the first Sunday of every month. We are averaging between 12 and 20 people in attendance each Sunday.

The temperature was actually quite cool last night, and I climbed into my sleeping bag at the outset. The colonel's convoy arrived from Baghdad and she brought Carol Y. along. I was glad to see him because it confirmed that I'd be able to go back on the convoy to Baghdad on Tuesday and spend a few days at Ibn Sina.

I spent the rest of the afternoon showing him around, talking, and catching up. We discussed his life at Womack, and life down in

Baghdad. He gave me some insights into the types of patients they are seeing at Ibn Sina and what their workload is. It sounds very similar to the workload we had at Dogwood in the early days of the war. I am still curious to see for myself how things are operating there, and I look forward to the trip, if for nothing else than to just have a set of different faces to see. I think Carol is relieved to finally see what our hospital here is like and to realize that I have no interest in making a permanent switch. I have decided that I am quite content to stay here if we must spend another five months on this deployment. The living conditions are the best we've experienced on the deployment as a whole, and they are getting slowly better each week as more things are procured or added. He should enjoy the next few days as a break of sorts from the routine that he and Bill have in Baghdad.

Col P. showed us pictures of the hospital at Dogwood as it was dropped and either packed up or destroyed. Apparently all the tents, liners, and anything that is cloth or fabric will be burned because it would never be able to pass agricultural inspection on its return to the US. I found it hard to believe that the hospital was no longer standing. In the big picture it is no great loss, but we invested a lot of time and spirit into that structure. She also showed us photos of the UN building after the bombing attack. It was a devastating series of pictures. The main element of the 28th CSH ultimately treated all of the injured patients save one. It was, by their report, a busy few days but also a rewarding experience.

08 Sep 03 – Today, Carol expressed a rather interesting, fresh view about the CSH and the significance of what has been accomplished so far on this deployment. He said that if you stop and consider the numbers of surgeries that have been performed and how many patients have been seen and helped, you would conclude that we have been the most productive CSH in the theatre during this war and really during any conflict in the recent past. We trekked across 300 miles of enemy territory, set up a crucial hospital near the battlefield front, and performed admirably and beyond everyone's expectations. I wish that I could have put it into that perspective.

10 / Visiting Baghdad

10 Sep 03 – It is Wednesday evening, and I am now at the main element of the 28th that is set up inside Ibn Sina Hospital in Baghdad. Ibn Sina was a prominent Arab physician who played an important role in teaching the modern generations in this region about the practices of Hippocrates. He is very well respected among the Arab people. The hospital is located in an area of Baghdad near the main Presidential palace located beside the Tigris River. The entire surrounding zone is secure and contains other headquarter buildings. The hospital itself was used for high ranking Iraqi officials and other people who found favor with the prior regime. It is beautifully constructed with liberal use of marble for the flooring and walls, but it is somewhat run down in many areas from neglect. There was minimal damage during the war phase because it was secured early and the looters were prevented from doing too much damage. There are several computer terminals missing from some of the medical equipment, but overall, the facility was in good shape.

After another beautiful night in Tikrit two nights ago – in which the temperature dipped into the 60's – we left there around 0800 and traveled into Baghdad without incident. During the trip I rode in the open backseat of the commander's Humvee. On the ride I noticed two things I had not seen before; a train running along a track that paralleled our road and many Iraqis out planting crops in gardens of all sizes along the road. I am not sure what all the crops were, but I did notice what looked like short corn and many grape vines. There were multiple vendors along the roadside selling the grapes and other fruit that I didn't recognize. After arriving just before noon yesterday, I spent the rest of the day being toured around the hospital and surrounding area. The first thing I noticed in Baghdad was that everyone was wearing the soft uniform cap instead of the hard Kevlar. I later learned that Kevlar is still worn if riding in a vehicle or if leaving the safe zone. The other thing I noticed was that it was several degrees hotter.

It was good to see Bill and the other guys again, and they have made a great effort to make me feel welcome. I cannot help, though, but feel like I am the country cousin that has just come into the city. In looking at my uniform and soft cap and rucksack, I notice that they are all dusty and showing more wear and tear than what I see here. The first place they took me was for lunch at a "local" Iraqi restaurant down the street from the hospital. They treated me to a fast-food lamb burger. The flavor was good, and it is now almost 36 hours later and I have not suffered any illness. The canned drinks were very cold and refreshing in the heat.

After lunch, Bill and I stopped by the 30th Medical Brigade headquarters across the street from the CSH to confirm the details of our lecture. We then returned to the hospital, where Bill continued my tour of the facility. It was good to see all the familiar faces from Dogwood. There were also several new faces around who have come in as replacements.

At dinner last night, I noticed that they are lagging behind our facility in Tikrit in terms of their food selection and quality. They are still eating the Army rations instead of the food from Brown & Root. I mentioned that our meals were different but didn't feel the need to elaborate. Their living quarters are divided between two dormitory-type buildings. The officers live in the building that is connected to the hospital, while the enlisted soldiers live in a building on the other side of the hospital. Bill and Carol have a room on the third floor of the four-story building and share their room with Jerome P. They are sleeping on their cots, but almost everyone has a sleep pad and other cushioning. Each room has a window with an air-conditioning unit, a sink, and a large metal cabinet. They have also bought an area rug from one of the local vendors to place on the tile floor. They share three common bathrooms with the other rooms on the floor. The bathrooms contain a toilet that has only low flushing pressure, a shower stall, and two sinks. In most any condition, it is superior to the LSA at Dogwood.

After dinner I enjoyed just hanging out in various rooms and catching up on the events that had transpired since we were all together at Dogwood. I spent the most time talking to Matt B., Bill, Cal, and Shaun N., a replacement surgeon from the 10th CSH. Later in the evening, we all went up on the roof of the building and enjoyed the very pleasant Baghdad night while smoking a cigar. There were many high-rise buildings visible both across the river and back in the other direction. Everyone told me that they feel relatively safe here within the "Green" zone, but they can occasionally hear gunfire at night and see many flares off in the distance. Afterwards, I slept in air-conditioned comfort on a clean cot after having taken a shower just before bed. It was a nice improvement over what I am accustomed to, but in a way, it was almost too nice and is taking me out of the rustic frame of mind that I have for living in Tikrit.

This morning I attended a morning report at 0730 that they hold in the medical library just down the hall. The library is a large room with two conference tables, not unlike rooms that you would find at hospitals back in the US. The meeting this morning was made all the more unusual because there was a reporter and camera crew there from ABC news filming a story about the types of patients we are treating here at the CSH. The focus of this story will be on the patients, but several of the physicians were followed for part of the morning and gave comments to the reporter to be used in the story. The story may air as soon as this evening – Wednesday – on the east coast.

At 1000 Bill and I met up with two staff officers from the 30th Med Bde who took us over to the Convention Center for our talk at 1100. We presented our talks to a group of physicians from our CSH and from local Baghdad hospitals and medical schools. I estimate there were around 35–40 Iraqi physicians in the audience, including the Iraqi Minister of Health. We each spoke for 45 minutes with a 15-minute question session. At the end we both received very complimentary remarks and fielded several questions from the audience, which reinforced our opinion that our topics were well received. I have decided to now declare myself an international lecturer and list that as an accomplishment on my resume.

The questions continued in an informal manner after the official session concluded, and then we traveled back to the hospital. I spent the afternoon walking around the hospital visiting with old friends and generally relaxing with the pressure of the lecture now behind me. I am on call tonight and will see how medicine is practiced here compared to Dogwood and Tikrit. My hunch is that it will not be very different.

12 Sep 03 – My call night was very uneventful with only one admission, a 21-year-old Pakistani worker at one of the local DFAC's who had recurrent abdominal pain. He was stable by the next morning, and I released him with minimal testing and treatment because nothing really seemed indicated.

At 1645-yesterday afternoon – which was 0845 EST – we held a memorial service for the events of September 11th. COL P. presided and was joined by the chaplain for additional comments. I will give the colonel credit, as she did a good job of reading prepared remarks about the significance of the day and the impact it had brought to all of our lives. She told the story of speaking recently with one of the Iraqi interpreters who is working here. He told her that the majority of Iraqis who despised the Hussein regime believed that Allah had worked through the United States to liberate them. This brings up the idea that no matter how devastating the attacks of September 11th were to our country, without them, we would likely not be here now and the Iraqi people would not have tasted freedom.

I still vividly remember where I was when I heard of the first plane crash on that morning and how I was watching the live coverage when the second plane crashed into the south tower. Our lives and our children's lives in the US will never be the same because of the events of that morning. Now we are finding out how the impact of that morning is reaching other people throughout the world. In the case of the citizens of Iraq, I think they will ultimately be thankful for the liberties that they are being provided.

This morning after rounds, Bill and I saw two patients in the ER with cardiology issues. The first was a young soldier who was having an irregularity of his heart rhythm that neither Bill nor I had ever seen before. We gave him some advice about stopping a new vitamin he had started taking recently and a prescription for a beta-blocker to slow the heart rate down. The second was an Iraqi EPW who had valvular heart disease and a nice murmur to hear. He was stable from a cardiac standpoint and didn't need to be admitted, but it was just nice to talk cardiology again with a colleague.

Later in the morning, we walked outside the hospital complex and went around exploring the area. Bill took me by the PX and gym that were about a half-mile away. The gym was a nice facility, while the PX was a small trailer with not much of a selection. Next we climbed a tower with over 200 steps that is located beside an old bombed-out Republican Guard building. Once at the top of the tower, we were afforded a nice 360-degree view of the city, and I took several pictures to document certain landmarks, including the crossed sabers and the Tomb of the Unknown Soldier. After climbing back down the circular stairway, we explored a bit more around the bombed out building and took some more photos at ground level. After walking back to the hospital, Bill took a nap, and I organized the photos and saw some consults in the ER and the Outpatient Clinic.

It is now after dinner, and I can say that the piece of meat/steak that they served me was the worst that I have seen in a long time. The mashed potatoes were tolerable – I've eaten mashed potatoes for four straight nights – but the broccoli with cheese casserole was not edible. Overall, the quality of the meals here is poor, and I joked with Bill that I'm starving to death here and that I need to go back to Tikrit to get something decent to eat.

Last night we watched a segment from the series called "Band of Brothers." We all agreed that we really don't have that much to complain about in terms of our living conditions compared with what the soldiers went through in the infantry in WWII. Perspective, in tolerable doses, is a useful sentiment to have.

I am a bit excited about something the commander told me earlier in the week and then confirmed for me yesterday. She denied my request to have the Army pay for me to return to the US in November to attend a medical meeting in San Antonio, but then immediately told me that I could attend the meeting if I was willing to pay for the trip. I have the option of trying to fly space available and take my chances or go ahead and purchase a ticket from Kuwait back to the US. The unit would get me to Kuwait and then I'd be on my own, which is fine. I have learned that things on deployments often don't occur as announced, but I am being cautiously optimistic that I can pull this trip off and be able to see Ana and the kids for a few days.

13 Sep 03 – It is late Saturday night, and I am just about ready to go to sleep. It has been a good day filled with many small accomplishments. My call period last night was very light and included only one admission. I was able to connect to home via the Internet at 0400 this morning and "talk" via instant messaging with Ana and several friends she had over to host a mid-tour party in my honor. It was good to read the messages and know that everyone back home is thinking of me and thinking of our troops here. I think it must be hard for our families to keep up the intensity of worrying about us and be constantly thinking about us.

We were able to be on the Internet for around 90 minutes and I think everyone was satisfied with the interaction. It was certainly better than we could have accomplished with a phone call. Being a little tired from getting up so early, I went back to the room to take a nap and slept until past noon. It was a very good feeling to sleep in an air-conditioned room and know that I had no real responsibilities or obligations I needed to meet because Bill was on call.

Just prior to afternoon rounds, a group of congressmen from several southern states arrived to tour the hospital and visit with some of the wounded soldiers. I saw a representative from Virginia and South Carolina, but none from North Carolina. Of course, they were traveling with a large entourage that included reporters and TV cameras filming them as they walked along. They stopped us on rounds and chatted for a short time but then continued on with their visit. I don't believe I was ever captured on film as a supporting member in the background. Bill said that this is not an unusual occurrence here because this is a fairly high-profile hospital now, even more so since it is the only one in Baghdad. I think I am ready to go back to Tikrit, where the medical practice is a great deal more laid back. I don't need all the exposure they seem to have here.

Tonight a group of us caught a shuttle to the Al Rasheed Hotel that is located across the street from the convention center where our medical conference was held. We ate dinner in an Iraqi restaurant where they actually had glasses and tableware and porcelain plates. It struck me how much I missed those simple features of a routine meal back home. They also served fresh bread and salads that were very good. I ate the lamb kebobs and capped the meal with ice cream and coffee in a real cup and saucer. It was amazing how good it felt to act like a civilized person at a meal again.

In the lobby of the hotel, we again ran into the congressional group, but this time without the cameras and the hoopla. Two of them actually stopped and chatted for a few moments before being whisked away by all the handlers. After we saw the group, it made more sense to us why we had seen several men walking around outside the restaurant wearing earpieces and carrying unusual looking weapons. We then walked around the shops a bit and caught the shuttle back to the hospital. We finished our evening with another cigar on the rooftop looking out over Baghdad.

11 / The Return to Tikrit

15 Sep 03 – It is after dinner, and I am back in Tikrit having arrived this morning on a Blackhawk, and yes, it remains a very fun experience. Today was even more fun because I flew in a position facing forward near the window – as opposed to facing backward in the standard medevac configuration – and I was able to see much better than ever before. It was a beautiful morning, and I enjoyed the 55-minute return flight that I shared with several other soldiers who had been in Baghdad for one reason or another. When our helicopter landed, Carol was standing by. We shook hands and exchanged a brief word, and he boarded the aircraft for the flight back to Ibn Sina.

Yesterday was a good day. Bill and I attended a Contemporary Christian service, contemporary in that the music is mostly modern praise songs. It was a good service led by a very lively lieutenant colonel reservist chaplain who preached a message that was challenging to us all. Later in the afternoon, Bill and I joined a large group of Catholics as they walked to the Four Headed Presidential Palace for mass. It is currently the Coalition Provisional Authority (CPA) Headquarters under the direction of Paul Bremer, who is coordinating the civilian effort for the rebuilding of Iraq.

Although we weren't Catholic we enjoyed the opportunity to get inside the palace. The mass was held in a large ballroom labeled "chapel." It was very ornate, as expected, with a domed ceiling, marble floors, and two large murals. There was also a large golden chair that looked like a throne, and we all had our pictures taken in turn sitting in the chair. Behind the chair was a large mural of Iraqi rockets being launched.

The mass itself seemed like a standard ceremony to me and was fairly well attended. I saw LG Sanchez, who is the commander of the coalition forces task force in Baghdad, attending the mass. Afterwards we all left the chapel and joined the line to eat in the palace DFAC. That DFAC is supported by Brown & Root, and offered a choice of three different entrées, a salad bar, and a table with different types of fresh bread. I found it very interesting that the palace has such fine food when the CSH is still suffering through "A" rations. Needless to say, the meal was quite good, and we followed it by exploring around the palace. We soon found was the theatre room downstairs where they were showing AFN-Sports (Armed Forces Network). We watched ESPN Sportscenter for about half an hour before I decided I needed to get back to the hospital since I was on call. Many of the others stayed for hours watching football when the games came on. On our way out, Bill and I found the spectacular pool area and had pictures taken there.

Later we gathered again on the roof for one last opportunity at conversation and cigar smoking. My call night was quiet, and I had no further admissions. Cal and Matt B. attempted unsuccessfully early this morning to save a soldier who'd been attacked with a large caliber weapon that blew away a large portion of his abdomen. One of my impressions from my time there at Ibn Sina is that the trauma business is still a steady one, even if the internal medicine business is not very busy.

After a small breakfast I said goodbye to everyone, and we loaded onto the back of a five-ton truck for the short ride over to a main helicopter-landing pad. I was worried that with Secretary of State Powell in town and planning to fly north this morning, we might get bumped from our flight. Everything occurred on time and we were in Tikrit before the heat had a chance to rise. I am very content to be back, and everyone seemed genuinely glad to see me. I also think that Carol had a good time here and will more easily come back the next time to give me relief. I anticipate he will need to return in November if I can arrange the details to attend the Army American College of Physicians meeting in San Antonio.

17 Sep 03 – It is midday Wednesday, and I have spent the morning catching up on e-mail and helping the other docs orga-

nize our area in the Think Tank. We have recently joked that we are going to have a yard sale and see if we can make some extra cash. Drew recently built a small shelve unit that sits atop one of the tables to hold our movie collection. Last night he was inspired to build a bookcase. It stands over seven feet tall and would hold hundreds of books. We joked with him about its proportions, but we are glad to have a place to start stacking up the books and magazines that we are collecting.

Lee M. is the replacement orthopedic surgeon for Rob G., and he flew up on the flight Monday morning with me from Baghdad. He had arrived there just the night before and was quickly manifested to come north. He is a graduate of West Point and USUHS – the military medical school – and is normally stationed at Ft Eustis in Virginia. When we came off the helicopter, he was called into the OR to assist Rob on a case he was working on from that morning. Since then, they have done three other cases together, and I think he is grateful for Rob still being here to orient him until he gets his bearings.

The weather has been noticeably cooler since I returned from Baghdad. I don't know if that is the trend there as well or if it is isolated to this area because of our more northern position. Either way I am satisfied and enjoying the relief. We are still scheduled to receive our housing trailers next week, and while I was away we obtained the AFN (Armed Forces Network) converter box. I am told that Sunday night there was quite a crowd watching the NFL games. Yesterday morning there was a large crowd watching the Monday Night game, and yesterday afternoon I was able to watch a good portion of the tape-delayed NASCAR race from Sunday. I have been able to follow the ongoing race season very closely. Ana sends me NASCAR papers and I frequently visit NASCAR.com to read stories. Recently the web site began the Track Pass feature on NASCAR.com, which allows me to listen to the audio of the races and watch highlight videos. I talked to Bill early this morning, and they are still not able to get the AFN services.

I have settled back into my comfortable routines, and I have observed that there are several things I really like about this location compared to Baghdad. Even though it is dustier, I like the more rustic feeling. I guess I have grown accustomed to sleeping in tents with the flaps up and waking to see the sun rising above the distant horizon. I enjoy the smaller number of soldiers here and the lack of attention from the press and leaders of the higher headquarters. I feel as if we have a smaller family where we all know one another and keep up with what is going on with everyone on a daily basis. I also enjoy not having to be politically correct. I like our food, and I like our Think Tank. I like running in virtually any direction and not having to worry about being the target of a sniper. I like our open-spaced shower where I don't have to worry about touching walls. I enjoy our access to the Internet.

19 Sep 03 – Rob G's. chronic back pain finally made it necessary for him to return home for possible surgical correction. Last night we held a farewell party for him. There were pictures and a video, and many people shared their fond memories of him. Later in the evening, the physicians congregated in the sand behind our tents and celebrated his departure with some fine Cuban cigars. He then spent the majority of the night packing the remainder of his stuff for the flight today. I told him before he left that he is truly an original and that things will not be the same here without him.

His departure leaves Colin, Rob D., Drew, and me as the last original physicians of the group that came up here. I continue to remind myself that as the days pass, my time here is shorter. I have been somewhat distracted by getting settled back into my routine and by the possibility of traveling again in November. This has all worked in my favor because the time keeps passing by, and before I know it, spring will be here and I'll be redeploying for good.

12 / Acceptance

21 Sep 03 – Ana told me that Logan had scored a goal in his soccer game, and he was pretty excited about it. I was also pretty excited but tried to temper it somewhat in my mind so as to not become bitter about missing it. I am constantly reminded that there are things occurring in the lives of my wife and children – the most important people on this earth to me – and I am not there to share those things with them.

My overall mood has been surprisingly good lately, and I hesitate to take credit for that. I know that we can will ourselves into many attitudes, but I think there is Divine help that is causing my emotions to be more balanced. I constantly petition God to strengthen me and help me to find the blessings in this deployment, and I think He is trying to be true to my requests. The difference may be that I am finally beginning to let him. My mood about the length of the deployment is softening, and I'd like to believe that it is more than just being defeated by the oppression of the Army's machine.

Right now I feel like I've slipped into the acceptance phase, and I spend my time pursuing the things that I'd like to get accomplished instead of worrying about my battle against the Army. Regardless of how it has come about, I am happier, and it makes the passing days a little easier to tolerate. In fact, I think that the time is moving by at a better pace than it was before. Each day is a day closer to being home, and I feel the momentum slowly building since we have passed the halfway point. I know the holidays are just around the corner, and that I will be severely tested during that time. For now, I am more content, and that is sufficient.

27 Sep 03 – As planned, we held the Mid-deployment Luau

Party last night starting at 1900, just before the sunset. It was held on the basketball court outside the DFAC. Our nurse practitioners Theresa H. and Dianne S. led the charge in decorations and arrangements and were significantly helped by many others. They used items that had been mailed from home for the decorations, as well as things that were made. There were two large strings of outdoor lights extended between the basketball goals to provide a street-festival type atmosphere. As the sun faded in the west, everyone emerged with his or her best Hawaiian outfit. For most, that included a Hawaiian shirt and our black Army PT shorts. Others were more creative and had an assortment of homemade party wear. All were festooned with leis and were treated to little umbrellas in the fruit punch.

During the party we all shared turns drinking the grog, which is a mixed punch that is common at military functions. The tradition of the grog was explained as the different sections added each component. For instance, a thick red liquid chosen by the EMT section was added to symbolize the blood that had been shed by those who'd passed through our doors. The maintenance section poured some thick black liquid into the bowl to symbolize the oil that was used up in keeping our generators in working order. The chaplain added seawater to remind us of the ocean we'd eventually cross to reunite with our families.

And so on it went with everyone adding "edible or fit for human consumption" material to the punch bowl until we had created this Fear-Factor type mixture. Then the challenges went out to "drink the grog." Of course, my turn eventually came, and I tolerated the mixture until I came to some particulate material. That's when the tradition ended for me as I spit it out on the ground. Overall, the experience was hilarious, and some people actually seemed to relish the concoction. For me, it was a bit on the briny side, but at least I sampled it and lived to write about it.

We had borrowed a sound system with large speakers from somewhere on post, and the music started out with an island-related theme. For our entertainment, Rob D. and I both had large squirt guns that we used to ambush people all night long. Lest it seem that

I am totally childish, I'd like to establish that it was my wife who had mailed them to me along with the Hawaiian shirt and lei for this party. From my standpoint, it added just the right amount of fun and intrigue – stalking helpless victims and watering them down. I am actually quite surprised that I wasn't the target of a bucket of water. Everyone seemed to really enjoy themselves, and I remarked to several people that we really needed this party as a unit.

The powers that be were concerned about having this party in general and being out of uniform in particular. But others and I believed that a medical unit faces a unique stress in dealing with the daily decisions of life and death, and we *needed* a party like this to defuse the pressure. No other unit in the Army faces the exact type of pressure we do on a daily basis over such a long period of time. I did not believe that any of the other units on post would begrudge us that opportunity. To my knowledge, no one has objected to our party or the fact that we were "out of uniform" for a few hours.

The only unfortunate aspect about the party is that John L. and Lee M. spent 10 hours in the OR working on a soldier injured by an IED and were unable to enjoy a single minute of the luau. There were two other soldiers hurt in the attack, one of which went to Ibn Sina yesterday and the other that is stable and only required a washout of his wounds late last night/early this morning. All together, they were operating until 0430 this morning.

29 Sep 03 – Yesterday in church I learned about Rosh Hashanah and Yom Kippur. Rosh Hashanah celebrates God's creation and is the Jewish New Year. Ten days later Yom Kippur signifies the Day of Atonement – the day on which the High Priest would enter into the Holy of Holies in the Temple to offer the annual sacrifice to account for the people's sins. The application to Christianity is that we celebrate Christ's death and resurrection as the ultimate atonement for our sins, obviating the need for any other high priest besides Christ. I think that one of the strengths of having a multi-denominational congregation on this deployment is that I am exposed to other religious concepts and principles. In some ways it is like an ongoing laboratory session from a college class on Judaeo-Christian religions.

02 Oct 03 – It is midday here, and I am sitting alone in the Think Tank while the surgeons are all napping. They have had two busy days and nights and were all operating until 0330 this morning, caring for the soldiers injured by an IED near the entrance to the 4th ID headquarters at the palace in Tikrit. The attack happened late yesterday afternoon as the convoy approached within 300 yards of the palace gates. Of the four soldiers involved, we received two for treatment. Of the other two, one soldier was killed directly in the attack and the other was returned to duty without need for further treatment. When we heard of the injured soldiers, I went to the ER and waited with everyone else. Because there were only two incoming casualties I sat off to the side and observed the activity.

I remembered back to the early days of the war when we first set up our hospital down in Dogwood and was reminded of the excitement that accompanies any trauma that comes in, especially when the patients are US soldiers. There is an almost palpable buzz in the air when the radio identifies that the incoming patients are categorized as "urgent," which means that they need immediate attention. The big difference I see now compared to those earlier days in Dogwood is that everyone is still a bit on edge, but there is now an efficiency of movement and purpose that can only come through repetition and testing. Considering the overall experience between Dogwood and here, we have been tested and found satisfactory.

Last night as I observed, I saw a group of very dedicated and seasoned young men and women – officers and enlisted, physicians, nurses, and ancillary staff – who flawlessly went about the job of providing some of the finest emergency medical care available in the world, especially for a combat theatre. Aside from not having a CT scanner immediately available, we have the majority of the tools and expertise we need for initial stabilization of just about any possible injury. I was flooded with pride at being a part of this organization we call the 28th CSH-Tikrit.

Not long after the US soldiers left the ER last night, the MP's brought in two Iraqi EPW's who had just come into their custody earlier in the day. The MP's had received the EPW's on transfer from the new Iraqi Police agency that had apprehended them three days prior. One of the men was suspected as being an explosives device builder, while the other was thought to be one who plants the devices. While in custody with the Iraqi police, the EPW's had obviously been aggressively interrogated and were showing marked bruising. One of the men could be released after he was examined, but the other had more extensive bruising and was found to have a moderate degree of kidney failure. I admitted him and have been giving him copious amounts of IV fluid in hope that it will flush the proteins out of his blood and kidneys and allow his renal function to return to normal.

I am somewhat troubled because the condition this patient is in is due to the beating he has received. I am also troubled by the implication that he is responsible for some of the explosive devices that continue to injure and kill our soldiers and other innocent Iraqis, including children. I can say that this situation is where the rubber meets the road with the Christian principle of loving thy enemy and praying for them. At this point, my speaking interaction with him has been minimal, and I have been managing his care by orders in his chart. I know that there is always the possibility that the Iraqi police have falsely accused him, but it seems less likely. I need to pray for wisdom about preparing my heart and mind for dealing with him. In the meantime, I expect his injuries and renal dysfunction will require several days to heal and improve.

04 Oct 03 – It is late on Saturday evening, and I find myself sitting alone for the moment in the Think Tank. I'm not sure where everyone is now, but I bet they'll be back soon. The one thing that is a precious commodity here is solitude and privacy. I think that is one of the reasons why I have kept at my habit of running because it allows me to get away from everyone for about a half-hour, three times a week.

I have enjoyed the many soldiers I've met on this deployment and the stories they've had to tell about their lives back home. I haven't spent much time talking about theatre issues because I think that this hospital should be a sanctuary, a place for their minds to escape thinking about the hazards of their jobs here. I also think I have been able to put many soldiers' mind at ease when it comes to cardiac issues and fears. They seem pleasantly surprised to be talking to a cardiologist about their symptoms. Some of them have been having chest pains for a long time – even before deploying – and have never been able to talk to a specialist because their symptoms have not really warranted a referral. But here, they can tell their story, and I can reassure them and get them back to duty.

The EPW with renal failure is still here and is still showing signs of poor kidney function despite optimal supportive care. His mental status is normal, and he is, frankly, pretty demanding to our staff for someone who was just punished so severely by the Iraqi police. He is also exhibiting some dramatic tendencies such as holding his breath and writhing around when he wants attention. I anticipate that his kidney function will slowly improve over the next week or two, but there is always a chance that his condition could deteriorate. If he were to need hemodialysis, I honestly don't know where we'd send him. I don't know if they have that capability at the Tikrit Teaching Hospital. I have remained emotionally neutral toward him.

I spent some time yesterday being interviewed by an Army historian who is traveling around and recording the stories of soldiers here. He then will take the interviews back to the Army Medical Department Headquarters in San Antonio and have them transcribed and entered into an archive to tell the story of Operation Iraqi Freedom from the soldier's perspective. He said that ultimately the archives would be available for the public to be both heard and read.

06 Oct 03 – Yesterday morning we shared communion in the worship service in recognition of World Communion Sunday. By most accounts, it is a day that a majority of Christians in the world join together in community communion. It was also Yom Kippur, which is also known as the Day of Atonement. In the sacrificial system of the Old Testament, this was the day when the High Priest entered the Holy of Holies section of the tabernacle and atoned for the sins of Israel by pouring the blood of the sacrifice on the lid or mercy seat of the Ark of the Covenant. The sacrificial blood was needed to approach the Throne of God. These concepts still have meaning for modern Christians because we believe that Jesus,

in his role of High Priest, made the ultimate atonement or blood sacrifice when he poured out his own blood on the cross to enable all that claim that sacrifice to approach the Throne of God. Once and for all, the sacrifice was made and will never need to be made again. Through his blood we are forgiven, protected, and saved from destruction. I can't think of anything that has more significance than that.

The big news on the housing front is that they delivered the first two rows of housing containers to our LSA the other day. There are many more containers to be brought, and then it will be another week or two before the plumbing and electrical connections are made. Still most of us were relieved to just see the containers being placed. The temperature in my tent this morning was just barely above 60 degrees, so I think the containers are going to be ready at just the right time.

08 Oct 03 – At 2200 two nights ago, I found myself in the air between here and Baghdad International Airport (BIAP) accompanying a soldier with an arm amputation and shrapnel injuries. For the majority of the 40-minute Black Hawk helicopter flight, his condition was very stable, and I was lulled into a false sense of security. Shortly before landing, my situation rapidly changed as the oxygen tank driving the ventilator ran out of gas and needed to be changed. In ideal circumstances this usually poses no problem, and given the fact that we had a spare tank, I thought a standard switch would be uneventful. Unfortunately, when we connected the new tank the ventilator didn't respond like it had been doing for the entire flight up until that time. Again, that should have been no big problem because we can usually just ventilate the patient with a bag-valve mask. For some reason we couldn't get the mask to connect correctly to the endotracheal tube as the adapter had slipped off without us seeing it during the flight. As we struggled to open the spare mask and adapter, the patient's blood oxygen levels plummeted and his heart rate and blood pressure also shot up.

After two to three minutes of controlled panic, we were able to locate the adapter, connect the bag-valve mask to the tube, and start to vigorously ventilate him back to normal levels. By this time we had landed and taxied to the Air Force medical holding facility, and they were waiting to offload him. Once inside, I tried to relay the incident and assure them that, contrary to what the monitors were suggesting about his heart rate, blood pressure, and oxygen levels, he had been very stable during the flight.

I don't believe there will be any long-term consequences because his oxygen levels were decreased for only a couple of minutes, but it taught me a very valuable lesson about the management of ventilators in an air-evac flight. When I later tested the ventilator upon returning to the CSH, I found that it was functioning appropriately. I'm not sure what the problem was at the time that it was malfunctioning – maybe I pressed the wrong button and it wouldn't clear itself or something like that – but I will henceforth be better prepared for airway/respiratory problems when I'm in the back of an evac helicopter.

As we flew home I was lost in my thoughts, replaying the incident in my mind to see if I could determine the mistakes I'd made and not repeat them in the future. Before long, I found myself remembering my days as an Emergency Medical Technician (EMT) in high school and college when I would routinely find myself in the back of an ambulance with a patient as we rolled down the road on our way to another hospital. I marveled at the similarities, such as the feeling of vulnerability while you are temporarily isolated from the full spectrum of resources that are typically available.

I think that somewhere in those hours I spent in the back of an ambulance, I had the dream or vision of doing what I am now doing. Maybe not to the detail of having the specifics of being a cardiologist or being an Army physician caring for soldiers in a foreign country during a war, but I know I dreamed of being a physician with more knowledge and skills with which to make a difference. I don't think I allow myself to realize this often enough, but each day I practice medicine, it is a dream come true, no matter where it is or what the circumstances are.

We arrived back to the CSH safely, just before midnight. I didn't realize it at the time, but I guess the trip took enough strength out of me that I overslept the next morning.

Our overall admission numbers were decreased in September compared to the other months, as we admitted only 110 patients. Last night we experienced a new adventure as Camp Speicher came under a short attack by mortars that were fired from the highway that runs parallel to one of the boundaries. There were three mortars fired that made impact in unoccupied areas near the end of one of the distant runways. The first impact was fairly loud, but we all thought it was a planned detonation of unexploded ordnance, a common occurrence here. The second and third impacts happened shortly afterward, however, and we all rushed outside to see what was happening. We realized that this pattern of sound was distinct from the planned explosions.

The soldiers who went out to inspect the impact area said that the craters measured only about 1 meter in diameter, which means that the mortar was small in size. The typical technique is that the Iraqis have a mortar hidden in the back of a pick-up truck that comes to a stop long enough for someone to fire off the rounds, and then the truck moves along. It is an efficient way to fire the mortar, but it suffers from being a very inaccurate strategy for damage because there is no targeting step. It is more like a random drive-by. Apparently, the 21st CSH located down in Balad and the 4th ID headquarters located at the main Tikrit palace are routinely attacked at night, but they have sustained no serious injuries or damage in the time since the US has been here.

10 Oct 03 – My renal failure EPW improved to the point of being discharged back to custody this morning. He remained appreciative to me, and I was glad that despite my earlier reservations, I softened my heart toward him and tried to demonstrate the love of God to him. Some of the nurses later told me that he continued to be nasty to them making little explosion sounds as they walked by. I can't explain why he didn't act this way toward me unless he realized that he needed me to provide him with healthcare. One nurse said that one time a few days ago he made several of them uncomfortable when he seemed to taunt a soldier that had been admitted and had required an amputation of his arm. This behavior enraged several of the staff members, and I thought we were going to have

to move the prisoner to another part of the hospital to protect him from our staff.

The mood of our nurses, physicians, and aides is becoming bitter toward some of the Iraqi EPW's we see and treat, especially as we continue to read about ongoing ambushes on our soldiers. An Iraqi EPW who is accused of being a bomb maker, like the patient I just had, has almost no chance to receive sympathy. I feel the emotion, too, but I am working hard on channeling into a more loving approach. But, if I'd seen him smile at the sight of our injured soldier or heard him make explosion noises to me, I don't know if I could've maintained my compassionate attitude.

12 Oct 03 – Today has been one of the more unusual days that I've had in several weeks. I guess my day officially started early this morning when I awoke at 0200 and went into the DFAC to watch the NASCAR race happening live from Charlotte on the Armed Forces Network (AFN). When the race finished around 0530 my time, I came back inside the sleeping area in the Think Tank and laid down for what I thought was going to be a short nap. Being Sunday morning, I didn't need to worry about getting up at 0730 for rounds, but I thought I'd certainly wake up by church time at 0900. I guess I was more tired than I'd predicted because I didn't awake until almost 1100.

I was a bit guilty about missing church but then quickly realized that God knows the condition of my heart and will allow for occasional lapses. It felt really good to sleep inside the air-conditioned tent with the blankets pulled up around me for warmth. It also felt good to be a bit lazy and feel like I was truly sleeping in for a change. Even when I try to sleep in down in the tents on other Sunday mornings, the sun prevents me from sleeping too late. I think we are all becoming fatigued from working every day for the past 6 months without any reasonable breaks.

14 October 03 – I continue to be amazed at the poor communication system we have here in the entire theatre. I guess I expected that since we were the most technologically advanced nation in the world that some of that know-how would be present in our communication systems, but the challenge of making a field-capable

system has proven too difficult at this point. To make matters worse, there was no reasonable wireless phone system in Iraq prior to the war, and that service – like many other necessities – has been very slow in coming to most areas outside of Baghdad.

The other two areas that have been disappointing are transportation and supply. I have heard from others and read in historical accounts that these three issues are a recurring problem in every conflict or war that we have engaged in.

The supply issue is probably the one that impacts us the most and is the one that is potentially most harmful to our mission and our patients. There have been many instances of us not having the proper equipment to accomplish our task. We have now been functioning as a hospital in this location for four months, and just today I was annoyed to learn that a cardiac medication that I wanted is still not in stock after being ordered twice in early and mid-September. The medication in question is not an unusual one, and it is listed as being a part of our core formulary, yet we haven't been able to keep it in stock.

When I talked to our medical supply sergeant, I was less than satisfied that the Army's supply system had my patients' best interests in focus. I don't blame our supply personnel – I know that they are doing their jobs but are up against the supply system that no one can explain in a coherent or cogent fashion. Time and again we have only averted crises by having the critical item mailed from our hospitals back home, sometimes even using regular mail.

Yesterday afternoon I was summoned to the mortuary affairs compound near the CSH to pronounce a soldier who had been killed in an RPG attack earlier in the day. I didn't know all the details, and I really didn't need to in order to accomplish what I needed to do. Fortunately, there was only one black bag lying on the floor of the refrigerated container with an American flag draped over it. One of the mortuary affairs soldiers opened the zipper, and it was immediately evident that he had died quickly from exsanguination caused by the large diameter wound in the upper part of his abdomen. The projectile round had passed cleanly through him but in the process had severed his descending aorta, and his blood loss would have come very rapidly.

The process of pronouncing someone officially dead is not a topic that I ever remember covering in a formal way in medical school. It seems intuitive that as a physician you could easily make that determination. However, I remember the first time that I was faced with that scenario while I was doing my internship, having freshly graduated medical school. I was on call early in July and one of the nurses notified me that a patient I was covering that night had died and that I needed to come and pronounce him. After entering the room, I was suddenly struck that I didn't know if there was an official procedure that I should follow because no one had ever told me, and I hadn't foreseen the need to ask. In that situation, I did what I often did during my internship year, I asked the nurse because I felt she'd probably have the experiential knowledge that I needed. She told me that she'd seen it done every kind of different way but that the important thing was that I was able to complete the death certificate because no one is officially dead without a certificate. As time went by I learned the technique of common sense.

After leaving the black bag in the refrigerator, I walked back to the other tent to complete the death certificate. While verifying the soldier's identity by checking his dog tags and military ID card, I noticed the picture of the young girl in his wallet with the pleasant smile and relaxed look on her face. The soldier was 19 years old. In a situation like that, I cannot help but have a very short-sighted viewpoint and wonder what we are still doing here. Why are the Iraqi insurgents so intent on firing RPG's at our soldiers and placing IED's in areas that are going to kill others? I can't answer these and many other questions.

Carol Y. arrived back to Ibn Sina from emergency leave, and I think Bill has left on his parenthood leave. If COL G. gives approval for my Continuing Medical Education (CME) trip it will be cutting it close for Bill to return to theatre and have Carol come up here in time to replace me, but it can be done.

The surgeons had only two minor cases in the OR today, and we all had the chance to eat dinner together in the Think Tank. We've completed the first four seasons of M*A*S*H, and tonight we began our next series — Band of Brothers. At the conclusion of tonight's first episode, we were all struck by how much harder those men had it compared to what we are living through. We've felt sorry for ourselves a great deal on this deployment, but I think watching this series is going to be a good reality check for us all. My father served in the Pacific in World War II, and I know that there hasn't been a generation alive since that can compare to the caliber of men and women that fought in that war. That generation demonstrated the classic example, in my opinion, of facing challenges and persevering to accomplish what needed to be done. I am not sure that my generation could withstand the extremes that the soldiers of WWII endured and overcame. I hope and pray we never face those sorts of challenges again.

16 Oct 03 — Recently we admitted a teenage Iraqi patient who'd been involved in a MVA. For several days we had trouble finding his family to let them know he was fine and when they could pick him up. After exhausting all the avenues we knew, Salam — one of our interpreters — offered to go out and find them. Three hours later he returned with the boy's father, and there was an emotional, tearful reunion. Through the interpreter, the father said that he feared his son had been killed. He was extremely appreciative and happily left with his son. We later asked Salam how he'd found him, and he said that once he knew the father's name it was easy to learn where he lived by the word of mouth network in Tikrit.

Tonight there was another mortar attack by marauding insurgents. Following each mortar attack, we have seen and heard a response team firing large amounts of ammunition towards something both from the ground and from attack helicopters. None of the mortar attacks have come even close to hitting our compound, and we feel pretty safe. Camp Speicher is large and it is apparent that there is no targeting involved in the attacks.

20 Oct 03 — The presence of two seriously injured Iraqi patients has caused a controversial disposition issue to resurface. We don't think that the facilities are adequate in theatre to be able to perform the surgery they need. The controversy in the disposition of these

two patients is that they are friendly forces as opposed to EPW's. The instruction during this deployment has been that coalition forces should receive the same standard of care therapy that we afford US soldiers, which means evacuation out of theatre for services that aren't available here. For that matter, we are morally obligated to provide the same level of care to all the patients we see, including the EPW's. As far as we can determine, these two patients have done nothing to disqualify us from treating them as friendly forces while they are here and offering them movement to a facility that would be able to provide their definitive care.

From our front line perspective, we are dealing with the family members of these patients on a daily basis, trying to answer their questions and offer them some hope that we'll be able to provide a good outcome. It is difficult to convince the people of Iraq that we have their best interests in mind when they are being told that we can't give them the same treatment that we give our soldiers. In our way of seeing things, it is a simple solution – transfer the patients to whatever facility they need to be at to have the surgical corrections they need.

We feel this issue is one of many that are crucial in measuring how effective we are at winning the hearts and minds. Both patients are in serious but stable condition and can't afford to have too much time go by while this issue is decided. I am amazed, however, that we are in the seventh month of this war and this issue has not been resolved. I know that we are not the only hospital who is treating patients with this situation.

22 Oct 03 – It is evening in the Think Tank, and all is quiet. Everyone has scattered to tend to showers, exercise or both. I am sitting and writing after having spent the past hour in our mid-week Bible study, where we are studying the book of Matthew. The group that attends this gathering is essentially the same group of people that attend the Sunday worship and Bible study. Our group of believers is not large in number, but we are striving to minister to one another and lift one another up in our faiths. The prayer request time is always a blessing as we share our concerns about the needs in

our lives and have group prayer. A mid-week service is designed to be a "pick-me up" experience, and it usually serves its purpose.

24 Oct 03 – We heard a helicopter fly by our location, but it was low and going in the wrong direction from what we'd expect for a flight coming from the typical southern approach. Almost immediately we heard three successive booms that were progressively louder. The third one was the loudest and noticeably shook the ground and the walls of our tents. After we looked at one another, we grabbed our Kevlar's and ran outside – maybe not the smartest thing to do, but curiosity is a strong force – to see what was happening. By the time we got outside, there was nothing to see, and we returned inside to make our way to the ER because we expected the medevac flights to be arriving soon.

While we waited for the helicopters, the story evolved that the explosions we'd heard were from rounds landing between our compound and the airfield across the street where our medevac helicopters are based. There are three airstrips here on Camp Speicher – one that we are located beside and two more that are across the road that divides us from them. They all run parallel to one another and have varying lengths. There is a single control tower like you would see at a commercial airport that is located beside the road that separates our compound from the other two strips. By report, one of the rounds landed near another unit's containers, one was near the tower, and the final one was farther down, closer to another part of the distant airfield.

Later in the afternoon, two of the flight surgeons came by from the medevac battalion and described the craters that were created by the explosions. As of now, the leading theory is that we were attacked by rockets fired from portable launchers instead of mortars because of the size of the crater and the distance traveled by the round. They described the crater as being about 3–4 feet across and 2–3 feet deep, with a shrapnel spray pattern shaped like a cone that spread out from behind where the round entered the ground.

The days are rapidly becoming shorter, and I know that short days mean the approach of winter and the holiday season. People are decorating for Halloween, and there are plans for a costume contest and a Fun-Run for the morning of the 31st. Others are talking about their plans for Christmas and a secret Santa gift exchange. In between there is a 10K Turkey Trot being held here on Camp Speicher, and I plan to run in it. It will be my first ever distance race and I am looking forward to trying it.

26 Oct 03 – While I was reading, the ER alerted me that there was a civilian patient coming with a possible stroke. When he arrived, he was a 52-year-old Filipino contract worker who'd been found down and was only moderately interactive. The first thing we noted was that his blood pressure was extremely high at 240/130. After performing a quick neurological exam, we learned that he was not moving the right side of his body and wouldn't look to that side, signs that suggested a problem with the circulation to the left side of his brain. His chest X-RAY was markedly abnormal and showed a widening of the shadow in the center grouping of structures. This area contains the heart and large blood vessels such as the aorta and pulmonary arteries. The chest X-ray strongly suggested a dissection or tearing of his aorta. We administered a powerful IV medication to lower his blood pressures to a target level and prepared him to fly to Baghdad.

The medevac flight was quickly arranged, and we lifted off for the 45-minute flight to Ibn Sina. The weather and conditions were very favorable because we arrived in 35 minutes. I was happy to arrive safely and with the patient in relatively stable condition. We made the hand-off quickly, retrieved the equipment that we used to transport him, and then moved back to the waiting chopper for the return flight. While there I saw Pam H., who is a family physician I know from Womack that has come to join the CSH as an ER physician.

Once we were northbound again, I was able to relax and enjoy the scenery from the window. I had enjoyed our approach into Ibn Sina because we had flown low along the Tigris River for quite a ways and then banked hard over the Four Headed Palace to begin our final approach into the landing zone. On our way out we retraced much of the same route, and I was again struck by what a large and sprawling city Baghdad is. Sunday afternoon is like a workday for them, and given the late time of day, the freeways and streets were congested similar to what you would expect in a metropolis while people are leaving work to return home. There are scattered signs of damage to some of the streets and buildings, but overall, the homes are intact, the vehicles are moving, and the people are milling about. Looking down on Iraq from a helicopter, it is hard to remember that there is a war going on.

Early this morning, insurgents attacked the Al Rasheed Hotel on the edge of the Green Zone by firing RPG's into the upper floors. By the time I arrived, the ER had cleared out, and the few people who were wounded seriously enough had been taken to the OR. It is my understanding that there was one death – a senior officer who was waiting to leave the country after having recently given over his command.

Tomorrow is the beginning of Ramadan – or Holy Month – for Muslims, and it is kicked off with a special family meal tonight to prepare for the coming fast. Ramadan lasts for 29 or 30 days, depending on the cycle of the moon. It is a time that was commanded by Allah for all Muslims to fast during the daylight hours. In talking with Salam, one of our two interpreters, he shared with me that to truly observe the fasting they are supposed to avoid food, drink, tobacco, and unclean thoughts or actions. He says that all Muslims are challenged to become better people during this month, and even the evil ones are encouraged to cease from evil activities or attitudes. At the end of the month they have a large celebration called the Feast of Feasts to signify that the period of fasting is complete. Throughout the month, the emphasis is on spending time with the family and cultivating those relationships.

28 Oct 03 – This morning Carol called me and told me that he'd been told to prepare to come up here tomorrow on the commander's convoy to relieve me so I could go back to San Antonio for the CME meeting. I haven't gotten official word that COL G. has approved my request, but I don't think they'd tell Carol to come here unless the expectation was there that I'd be leaving.

13 / A Brief Escape

30 Oct 03 – Late yesterday morning, Carol arrived in Tikrit as part of the commander's convoy. I guess his presence confirms the approval of my request to return to the states. After nearly being blown away by a shamal in Tikrit prior to leaving on the convoy I am safely sheltered within the walls of the living quarters wing of Ibn Sina in Baghdad. We are still awaiting the final paperwork, but I've come to Baghdad to be a step closer in the process once it is completed.

31 Oct 03 – This morning the commander held a staff call and informed us that the threat level for Green Zone attacks had been elevated for the coming weekend. For that reason, as of 2400 tonight, all staff are going to be restricted to the immediate hospital compound, with the only exception being someone having official business across the street at the 30th Med Bde. Unfortunately, that includes no access to the palace, the DFAC down the street, the PX, the gym, and the pools. For me, it won't be a big issue because I'm here to work while I await Bill's return. For the people assigned here, this restriction severely alters their lifestyle.

The quality of food here is still inferior to the food that we receive in Tikrit, and if I stayed here long, I'd probably lose more weight. The morning here is beautiful because the sky is very blue with minimal clouds and the temperature is only in the low 80's. Earlier this morning, I was given my official clearance to leave the theatre to attend the conference and visit home. If Bill was back, I could literally leave on the next medevac flight. His wife, Shannon, wrote me an e-mail that he'd been able to catch a flight yesterday to Frankfurt, Germany. Once in Germany, he'll move down to Ramstein Air Base to catch a space-available flight back to Baghdad.

As of this morning, 61 of the 72 beds here are occupied, with the vast majority of those beds being taken by Iraqis. Sixteen of the 61 beds are ICU patients, and many of them are very seriously ill. That group only includes one US soldier, who was wounded in an RPG attack and will be included on the air-evac mission planned for tonight. That mission is a large one that will hopefully evacuate approximately 10 patients. With the increased threat levels, the emphasis is being placed on moving patients out as soon as it is medically feasible. The OR performed eight cases yesterday, and they have seven cases scheduled for today. There were two Iraqi trauma deaths yesterday; one from a gunshot wound to the head and the other from a gunshot wound to the pelvis, resulting in irreversible blood loss. The majority of the seriously ill patients are Iraqis who are recovering from trauma wounds and are being managed by the surgeons.

01 Nov 03 – We are over 12 hours into our security lock-down, and nothing suspicious has happened so far. I hope we are over-reacting to perceived rather than real threats. I walked with one of the other physicians, Russell D., down the street about ¾ of a mile to the closer DFAC for dinner. Russell is an OB-GYN physician who just joined the CSH from Ft Bragg as a replacement for one of the other surgeons. Interestingly, in talking for a short time we learned that our sons attend the same kindergarten class back home, and he and his wife had recently joined our church.

After dinner I went with one of the other physicians, Chuck M. – a cardiothoracic surgeon from Walter Reed Army Medical Center (WRAMC) – to the Halloween Party being held in an adjacent building on our compound. Several people had received costumes in the mail or had gone to much trouble to make costumes from materials found here. Most of us, however, went to the party dressed as deployed soldiers. As expected, the music was loud and appealed to a different age group than what I represent. After a short time there, we withdrew to the rooftop to enjoy a cigar and watch the nightlights of the city. Unlike prior times on the roof, I didn't hear as much small arms fire in the distance. Feeling relaxed and satisfied, I called it a night and went to bed after a rather short evening of festivities.

Since being here I have witnessed a steady stream of trauma patients coming into the ER. Several of them have not survived their initial injuries, and their care has stopped downstairs. Most others have survived to be taken to the operating room, and the numbers would say that anyone who makes it to surgery following a major trauma has a better than 66% chance of survival. For the US soldiers, our role is to facilitate their evacuation, while for the Iraqis; our role is to manage them until the time of their discharge or transfer.

The workload here is definitely greater than what we have in Tikrit, and the physicians here are doing a good job of keeping up the fight. I can see the tension in everyone's face from maintaining this type of pace for so long now, and I think it will only get worse as the time passes.

My time of departure is nearing. Bill called me from Ramstein and said he was expecting to get onto a flight later today that would bring him to Balad. Once we are sure he is en route to Balad, I may be allowed to leave on an evac mission tonight.

24 Nov 03 – Much has happened in my life since I last wrote in the journal. I am now back at the main 28th at Ibn Sina after spending 15 glorious days at home with Ana and the kids and attending the medical meeting in San Antonio. I was able to leave for BIAP shortly after noon on 02 Nov, and after a prolonged stay at the passenger terminal there, I was able to get on a space available flight to Ramstein, Germany. In short order I traveled to Dover AFB, Delaware, and finally boarded a commercial flight from Baltimore to Raleigh.

During my travel odyssey, I could have made a movie entitled "Planes, Choppers and Humvees." In the course of the almost four weeks since I've left Tikrit, I traveled in one Humvee, one five-ton truck, five military planes (C-141, C-5, C-130), two commercial jets, two airport shuttles, one rental car and a Black Hawk helicopter. And I still haven't returned to Tikrit. Hopefully, that last leg of my trip will occur tomorrow.

I awoke very excited on the morning of 2 Nov because I was scheduled to leave on a ground convoy going to the airport. Bill had phoned late the night before after arriving at BIAP, and he was due to ride a shuttle bus back to the CSH that morning, clearing me to go. Around 0900, while I was waiting for the convoy to leave, the morning plans changed rapidly as we received word that a Chinook helicopter had been shot down, and we were to receive at least 30 US casualties – condition unknown. Slowly all the available physicians arrived in the ER, and we waited until around 1000 when the first patients started to arrive. It quickly became clear that we were experiencing a true mass casualty event – that is, the number of seriously wounded patients exceeded our level of resources – and we began to have to make decisions about priority of care based on which patients seemed the most salvageable. Every physician, including me – and I don't normally care for trauma patients – was pressed into service and responsible for at least one patient. The ER was literally jammed to an overflowing status, and I was seeing my patient in a hallway.

My patient was awake but not too alert, and I suspected he had sustained some sort of head injury. He had a bruise over his right eye, and there was an asymmetry to his forehead on that side from soft-tissue swelling underneath. He also reported pain in his left thigh (from a fracture) and pain in his right ankle (from a fracture). There was also evidence of singeing of his eyebrows from the brief fire associated with the crash.

While my patient waited his turn to go upstairs to the OR, I walked around and noted some of the other patients. I don't recall ever having seen so many seriously wounded patients in one place. Every direction I turned, there were soldiers with life-threatening injuries that were being aggressively treated. In some cases, the surgeons were doing emergency procedures there at the bedside in an attempt to save the patient's life. There was an intense focus on two soldiers in particular, as the resuscitation was continuing while the administrative officers tried to hurriedly complete the medical retirement paperwork. If a soldier dies on the battlefield before reaching the medical facility, the surviving family members receive a one-time death benefit package. If, however, a soldier is medically retired before death, the surviving family members receive a more robust benefits package. I am not certain of all the rules, but I know that we usually make a strong effort to retire someone before their inevitable death, if at all possible.

After about two hours, we learned that all the expected patients had been brought to us already. I later learned that 16 US soldiers lost their lives as a result of this terrorist attack. Of that number, I am told that four soldiers died in our hospital – I witnessed two of them – and another soldier died later after reaching Germany. Against that backdrop, I boarded a five-ton truck for a ground convoy to BIAP. I never saw Bill that day, but he told me later that he'd caught a ride on a medevac helicopter bringing a patient to the hospital from another separate event. I arrived at BIAP at around 1400 and began what would be a 12-hour waiting period to board a flight for Germany. I had hoped to hop onto a medevac flight but was told that they were all full because of the number of patients from the Chinook crash.

Hearing that there were no other flights out of Baghdad until the next day, I dejectedly settled in to spend the night in the passenger terminal. Unexpectedly, an angel in the form of an Air Force sergeant intervened after overhearing my pleas to get onto the medevac flight. Somehow, he was able to get me a seat on the 0200 space-available flight to Ramstein that I'd been told had no seats. In my excitement I forgot to notice his name on the uniform, but I hope the look of absolute relief in my face will be reward enough for his good deed.

Roughly 40 of us crowded ourselves into web seats along the sides of a C-141 plane amongst the cargo and settled in for the six-hour flight to Germany. I was too exhausted, both emotionally and physically, to notice how cramped, noisy, and cold the flight was. I quickly fell asleep and awoke as we were landing in Ramstein in the early morning. After clearing through customs, I went into the terminal and learned that I'd be able to catch another space-A flight into Dover later in the day. That flight was also on a C-141 but was only partially full, and we were able to stretch out across several seats and relax with plenty of space. We were also given a meal on that flight – a box lunch that was purchased for $3.50 at the time of check-in.

We arrived in Dover in the mid-afternoon, and after a brief trip through US customs, I proceeded to the terminal where the military travel agents were able to arrange a one-way flight for me from Baltimore to Raleigh. Because Dover has no commercial airport, I had to quickly arrange for a shuttle ride to the Baltimore Washington International (BWI) Airport 90 minutes away. That hurdle was cleared, and in the early evening I found myself on a Southwest Airlines flight headed from BWI to Raleigh. I phoned Ana from the airport and told her to keep the kids awake because I was going to rent a car and be home in a little over an hour. Because of the uncertainty of me getting approval to come home, we had chosen to not tell them anything, and I wanted to truly surprise them that night.

The looks on their faces when I walked in were truly priceless. They were so stunned that none of them spoke for a full 10 seconds. Caroline finally screamed "Daddy, Daddy" and they all came rushing for hugs. I can only dream about what the final homecoming is going to be like based on my feelings during that reunion.

The next two weeks went by too quickly as I made a concerted effort to spend as much time as possible with Ana and the kids. My conference sent me to San Antonio (Thursday the 6th to Sunday the 9th), where I was pleased to see old Army friends and acquaintances while learning a few updates in cardiology. I gave a small talk to the group of cardiologists on Saturday and shared many photos from the deployment along with bits of advice about what to expect and how to better prepare. The highlight for me was having Nathan, my best friend from childhood; join me in San Antonio for a short visit. I eagerly returned to Fayetteville on Sunday afternoon and looked forward to the remaining days with family and friends.

I was able to take the kids to the movies and out to eat on several occasions. I was also able to spend time with each child on a school field trip or on a special "date" of their choice. On the second Saturday, Ana threw a party for me, uniting several friends from work and church, as well as Ana's mom, both sets of my aunts and uncles, and two cousins.

Probably the most important part of the trip was the time I had to spend with Ana. I miss her tremendously, and I was often reminded why. I think she is doing a spectacular job of keeping everything together and functioning in my absence. The real challenge for me was to come home and enjoy being there without trying to intervene too much in the areas that had changed while I was away. In some ways I was more of a guest or an observer, and I worked hard to not exceed that boundary. I know the homecoming after the redeployment will present even different challenges, but this one was probably a good peek into what to expect the next time.

Ana and I have a tremendous network of friends and family for support, and I never felt closer to them than during my time at home. Many of them called or came by, and I can't thank them enough for what they mean to my family right now. I look forward to redeployment when I can re-enter everyone's lives in a more tangible way. My only fear is that I won't be able to carry the principles home with me that I've learned to rely upon here. Already I've seen that the habits that were such a large part of my life here are harder to practice and maintain at home when I'm put back into my other life. For me, that means I'll just have to work harder at the discipline needed to maintain my Scripture reading, prayer time, and exercise patterns when I return home for good.

Since returning to Ibn Sina, I have enjoyed the time with Bill, and we realized that we hadn't seen each other since September, when I came down to give the lecture. He had a good visit at home with his wife Shannon, their daughter Libby, and their new son, John Henry. He's a little chunk and looks great in the pictures that Bill brought back.

14 / Away from Home for the Holidays

25 Nov 03 – After spending the night on call to give Bill a much needed break, I awoke just in time to attend the 0645 convoy briefing for our planned trip back to Tikrit. We gave brief farewells and departed Baghdad shortly after 0800 for the first segment of the trip up to Balad. We stopped at our sister CSH, the 21st, and were met by a convoy that had originated earlier in the morning from Tikrit and included Carol, who was trading places with me and coming back to Ibn Sina. It was good to see him, and he told me that he'd actually had a good time in Tikrit during my absence. While we waited for our convoy to leave again for Tikrit, I went inside the 21st CSH to visit my friend Tamara M., who's an ER doctor there. She was surprised and pleased to see me, and we quickly caught up with each other over a cup of coffee.

We eventually left Balad for the rest of our 2 and ½ hour trip back to Tikrit. I didn't think I'd ever be glad to be in the back of a five-ton truck again, but I learned that in November, the back of a covered five-ton truck is more desirable than a snazzy looking Humvee that is missing doors. The weather remained overcast, and by the time we pulled through the gate onto Camp Speicher, a steady rain had begun. I remember laughing at the concept of "the rainy season" in Iraq, but I am now becoming a believer. Although my arrival back at the CSH occurred without much fanfare, I received a large number of hugs and "welcome backs." Our little slice of shared misery in Tikrit has truly evolved into a family. One of the things that I decided while I was home was to embrace the family concept here, and that is what I plan to do. I was honest and told everyone that I could not say that I was happy to be back, but that I was excited about our last three months together.

There have been several changes since I left. The first significant change is that the engineers on post have installed plywood floors in our hospital. Fortunately, they did most of the hospital before the rains began, and it has helped avoid flooding in our clinical areas. The net effect is that the floor has been raised slightly less than four inches, and we must now stoop slightly in several areas to avoid hitting the doorways and the heating plenum. That sacrifice is a small price to pay for having dry floors.

The second major change is that we have finally moved into the containers in the LSA. The bathroom/shower trailers are still not available because of some final plumbing issues, but the old shower tent is in use, and there will always be the porta-potties. As a matter of fact, once I was settled a bit, I visited the shower tent to knock off the road grime, and it was a sublime experience because the water was steaming hot and plentiful and the changing area was now heated. Afterwards, it was a nice change to be able to return to the trailer and have a clean place to hang my towel and store my clothes. We have 36 trailers that are housing two people in each, and my roommate is Rob D. There is ample floor space for each person, and the units have a built-in climate system, overhead lighting, and multiple electrical plugs. Our first mission is to buy a cheap rug at the PX to soften the linoleum floor a bit and make it homier.

26 Nov 03 – I fell asleep last night to the sound of hard rain against the roof and walls of the trailer, and for a while it was easy to forget where I was. I awoke later than usual for my normal routine here at 0700 and found that the day was still overcast with rain still falling. My sleep pattern has not returned to normal, likely due to multiple reasons including the change of time zones after my trip home and the depression that I've felt since returning. I believe my sleep will improve with time as the wounds of leaving my family again slowly heal and I slip back into my earlier Tikrit lifestyle. I am comforted by the fact that the days are slipping by again and that each day is one day closer to returning home with the target date for redeployment in the 3-month range.

28 Nov 03 – It is Friday morning, the day after Thanksgiving, and I'm sitting in the Think Tank trying to get organized. The sun is

shining today – finally – and my hope is that it will dry up some of the moisture that is lingering in the air, the ground, and in our tents/containers. I am still surprised by the change in the weather because I never would have believed there could be this much moisture in the desert. I am just thankful that the wooden floors were installed in the hospital – because we'd have some seriously soaked boxes of personal items – and that we've moved into the trailers to live. All is not ideal with the trailers, however, because we are currently without power in 12 of the trailers as a result of an Iraqi generator failure last night. The broken generator is apparently a serious challenge to us because the whole trailer system is under contract and must be serviced by the civilians who may or may not be working today because it is the Muslim Holy day.

Yesterday was Thanksgiving here, and we all were allowed the time for rest and reflection. Having recently returned from home it was a little easier for me to keep my mind in an attitude of gratitude than some of my other colleagues, who haven't been anywhere. However, I did not hear any significant negative comments throughout the whole day about being here. I think everyone did a good job of focusing on the positives and that made the day a very tolerable experience.

The 4th Aviation Brigade (of the 4th ID) sponsored a 10K Turkey Trot yesterday morning that ten of our members took part in. I had previously wanted to run, but I was out of shape from being home. Instead, I got up early and ran my normal route here at the CSH. Those who ran in the Turkey Trot had a good time, and three of the ten placed in the top three in their age groups, and one of the three, Michelle R., who is our new head nurse in the ER, was the top female overall.

We had five-ton trucks shuttling back and forth to the DFAC every thirty minutes, and the physicians broke into two groups to eat and provide coverage. I went in the second group and was duly impressed by the spread awaiting us. The DFAC is large but was nonetheless crowded, as soldiers from all over Camp Speicher came to gorge. I think all types of meat were represented: turkey, ham, pork, roast beef, shrimp, and tuna salad. The side items were mashed potatoes, dressing, and corn on the cob, multiple types of salad, bread, and cranberry sauce. For dessert there was pumpkin pie – which had a funny taste – pecan pie, chocolate cake, lemon cake, and a mixture of seasoned nuts. There was also eggnog that was a bit weak, coffee, juices, and soft drinks. For the evening meal they served steak, lobster, and crab legs, but by then I couldn't even think about eating that much.

In the afternoon, those who could exert more effort than sleeping played a flag football game. It was a spirited affair involving officers and enlisted on pre-arranged teams. The field was a bit soft and muddy, but the competition was fierce, and I think everyone had a really good time playing and watching. As darkness fell, everyone cleaned up and came back to the hospital where we, the physicians, were having an "Open House" in our area and serving appetizers and desserts. We thought it would be a good opportunity for everyone to socialize, and it served the ulterior purpose for us of getting rid of much of the food that we had stored in boxes.

After our affair we all headed over to our DFAC, where the TV was showing the Lions-Packers Thanksgiving football game. It was during that game that we first learned of the President's visit earlier in the day. We were all shocked and surprised and very pleased by his effort. Most soldiers hold President Bush in very high regard and today's trip only served to solidify that opinion. Having recently flown into the Baghdad airport (BIAP) under tactical conditions with the lights totally blacked out, I can say that what he did was quite risky.

My mood is continuing to improve each day, and I had a good night of sleep last night. During an Ecumenical Service yesterday at our chapel, I had a period of time to reflect on what I am thankful for. Aside from the standard, expected things like family, friends, and health, I also decided that I am thankful for being here in Iraq. This is because I know that I have learned things – and am learning things – here that I wouldn't have learned at home. It is easy to overlook the issues of personal growth when you are caught up in a lifestyle that involves being a husband, father, and employee. Here, all that has been reduced to a more fundamental situation, and through the physical and emotional struggles, I have learned to depend upon God and God alone. The biggest challenge I foresee in redeployment is applying that knowledge to the life I have back home.

30 Nov 03 – The blown Iraqi generator is still broken, and the air temperature seems to have fallen even more at night. Last night felt particularly cold because of the moisture in the air. In fact, sleeping in the trailer is probably not unlike sleeping in a meat locker, and I made the decision today to move my cot into one of the tents that has an ECU with heat. I have no way of knowing how long it'll be until the Iraqi generator issue is resolved, and I'd like to think that I've learned to not suffer foolishly when a reasonable solution was available.

Some people also received some mail today, which is a morale-lifter. Our mail service has slowed considerably in the past seven to ten days. A missile hit a civilian cargo plane shortly after take-off from BIAP. As reported in the news, the plane was able to land safely, but that attack has caused a great ripple of concern with the cargo carriers. This is significant because these civilian carriers bring much of our mail back and forth to Iraq, and it will certainly delay the service if they can't safely fly in and out of BIAP. All of these challenges with mail couldn't come at a worse time, as Christmas approaches. I know for me, I have not received at least two packages that Ana said she mailed before I came home for leave.

02 Dec 03 – We have officially dropped into double digits in terms of the number of projected days left on the deployment. As of yesterday we'd been in theatre 265 days, so that means that we have 99 days left until we hit our one year anniversary, the all-important milestone for units on this deployment. There is always the possi-bility that we'd be able to fly out before 10 Mar 04, but at least we shouldn't have to go beyond that day.

The weather here has been decidedly like winter, with cool tem-peratures and cloudy skies. I have slept better (warmer) the past two nights after moving into the tent that is heated. We are still await-ing the Iraqi contractors to fix the broken generator. All my posses-sions are still in my trailer, and I go there to change, but I come back to my cot in the tent to sleep. Each night there have been one or two others who have moved into the heated tent for the same reasons.

I saw two consults earlier today, but I have spent the afternoon helping Rob D. and Brennan C. adorn our area with the Christmas decorations we've received to this point. Ana mailed me a small artificial tree that I've put on our tabletop. Rob also received a small tree and several boxes of ornaments. We've used all the ornaments that our small trees needed and have hung the rest from the ceiling of the canvas lining of our tent with suture. We hung them at varying heights, and they look not unlike an ornament star field. I had previously hung two strings of American flag lights that Ana had sent me. While I decorated my tree I played some Christian seasonal music, and it helped me to get into the mood. The only thing missing was the eggnog, and I could've felt almost like I was home. I know that the Christmas experience is going to be painful and challenging, but I am resolving to work hard to minimize the negative and look for the meaningful.

The other thing I did last night was beginning to work on our annual family Christmas letter. When I finish my draft I'll e-mail it to Ana, and we'll edit it together as needed and then print it out there for inclusion into our Christmas cards. When you stop and think about it, it is quite amazing how I have been able to remain a part of our family's traditions through e-mail photos and letters. I certainly believe we've benefited more on this deployment from technology than any other soldiers in history, at least as it applies to staying in contact with our families. Taking advantage of this technology is one thing that I won't apologize for.

04 Dec 03 – It is evening here, and everyone is gathered around our table in the Think Tank. Anyone who came into our area would think that we're all working for a telemarketing agency or something similar because we all have headphones on and are staring at our laptops open in front of us. I'm working on my journal while everyone else is watching a DVD program.

The volleyball season has continued in repetitive cycles since July but is now on hiatus and has been replaced by soccer. Needing an activity to replace the running I've avoided lately because of the lower temperatures and late sunrises, I signed up for the ICU soccer team. Today was our first game, and we played against the OR team and won. We relied heavily upon some ringers from other teams we'd recruited at the last minute because we were short players. The games are two twenty-minute halves of continuous play with a ten-minute break in between. I did not anticipate being so winded after playing the first half, but I think it was just a matter of de-conditioning, and I think it'll change as we play more. The running was exactly what I was looking for, and it was fun. However, I can already tell that tomorrow will be a challenge from a movement standpoint. I've already self-medicated with Motrin.

I had to wait about 45 minutes for the showers to open, but when the hot water hit me it was almost a religious experience. It felt so good that I didn't want to ever get out, but I began to worry about first-degree skin burns. Our trailers are still without power – which is becoming very frustrating because I'd like to move out of the tent that has all the other people in it and be united again with all my possessions. Apparently the Iraqi contractors came yesterday and brought another generator, but when they started it up it wouldn't produce enough power to be effective. Now we have two large Iraqi paperweights where there should be one useful generator.

Jimie is a female general surgeon who recently joined us. She had her first trauma patient yesterday since arriving here. Unfortunately, she also experienced her first surgical death here. The patient was an Iraqi male who'd been shot for illegal activity near Samara – where the recent attacks and battles have been so brutal – and flown here in critical condition. Upon arrival it was obvious that he'd lost a significant amount of blood from a gunshot wound to his left flank, and his systolic blood pressure was barely in the seventies with a normal value being over one hundred in most men. In the OR they opened his abdomen and were met with a rush of blood that continued until he'd literally exsanguinated in front of their eyes. Eventually, they were able to see that the internal organ injuries were extensive and included the spleen, stomach, liver, intestines, and some of the major arterial branches off the abdominal aorta. The damage was so extensive that they couldn't get control of the bleeding in time.

07 Dec 03 – Today is a very special day because it's my birthday. I welcomed the day at midnight last night by enjoying a Cuban cigar outside the tent I've been sleeping in. The temperature was cool but not unbearable, and the sky was clear, providing me with another amazing desert star show. I reflected back to my fortieth birthday party a year ago when I shared cigars on my back deck with many of my friends. Wow – how things in my life have changed since then.

After a good night's sleep, I was able to sleep in until 0800 – it was Sunday morning and we weren't having rounds. We were all in a celebratory mood this morning because it was John K.'s first Sunday back from leave, and his chaplain's assistant had beautifully decorated the chapel. The songs we sang were all Christmas carols, and John spoke about the Advent Season – which is not heavily emphasized in the Baptist Church – and about the significance of Christ's fulfillment of prophecy in coming to this world. Following the sermon we participated in communion. After the worship service, we continued our study of the Book of Revelation by reading and discussing the sixth chapter, which deals with the opening of the Seven Seals that cover the scroll of God.

At the end of Bible study, everyone sang for my birthday, which was somewhat surprising because I had made a point of not mentioning the day. It was, nonetheless, a nice gesture, and my family away from home warmed my heart. Shortly following lunch, I was in the Think Tank when many of the physicians, nurses and various staff members came in carrying a cake and singing for me. The cake had been baked by Liz C., one of the OR nurses, in a bread-maker. It was a yellow cake with chocolate frosting that was reminiscent of the cakes that my grandmother would bake for me as a child. Adding to that wonderful memory was the fact that this cake was still warm, as was the frosting. I remember begging my grandmother for permission to eat it as soon as possible after she took it out of the oven, and that is still my favorite way to eat cake, regardless of the flavor. After singing, they all lingered a bit and shared the cake with me.

When they asked for a speech, I shared my story about the

comments I'd made with my friends and family last year as I'd celebrated my fortieth. I recalled how I'd said that I wanted something significant to happen to me in the coming year that would match the significance, in my mind, of turning forty. There is no doubt that this deployment qualifies as that event.

At around 1500 here, I was able to reach Ana and the kids by our computer phone connection. They had just gotten up, and I joked with Ana that it was a little unusual that I'd have to call them on my birthday instead of the other way around. In this case, it seemed acceptable since there is no easy way for her to pick up the phone and dial Iraq. I am just continually thankful that we have this technology available. The kids were all excited to wish me their best, and we made some plans for how we'd celebrate when I redeploy. Noah is excited that they'll likely celebrate his birthday at Disney and Caroline is excited to have another fancy-type little girl party. Logan is excited about the fact that I'll likely be home for his party this year if all goes well with the redeployment. I think that will go a long way towards making up for the one I missed last year.

As the afternoon wore on, I continued to revel in the significance of the day. Outside the weather was cool yet dry, and there was more crispness in the air than in days prior. The sky remained cloudless, and around 1700, before afternoon rounds, I went outside to see the sunset. I was treated to one of the most beautiful ones that I've seen on this whole deployment. For once, the horizon was free of clouds or haze, and the intensity of the late fall sun is such that I was able to look directly at it once it reached a position about twenty degrees above the horizon. From there, I watched as it slowly dropped toward the distant line. It appeared perfectly spherical and was an amazingly intense and rich orange color. The surrounding atmosphere seemed to radiate with a numerous shades of red, orange, and pink. It was definitely the kind of majestic event that was painted with brush strokes from a color palette that we cannot comprehend. I have mentioned before in my journal of times in my life that I classify as an event that I'll not easily forget – and this sunset will be remembered as one of them.

09 Dec 03 – This afternoon I was again treated to a spectacular

sunset, and then after the sun had disappeared, I turned to the east and saw an intoxicating moon. This phenomenon was the opposite of the morning when I clearly saw the moon in the northwestern sky after the sun had risen on the southeastern horizon.

My muscles have been quite sore in the past few days, as I have been playing more soccer in our small league. I'd hoped that the soreness would have resolved by now – and I think it eventually will – but its lingering reminds me that I just had another birthday. Obviously, I am not capable of simply going out and running around anymore without some preparation in the form of stretching. I am not very experienced in playing soccer, having only done it in my school years during physical education sessions, but I'm enjoying the exercise and competition it's providing.

I've been back in my heated trailer for the past two nights, and so far the power has remained on. The next step in improving the LSA is to get the shower trailer up and running such that we can take showers as needed and not be restricted by certain, often inconvenient, hours. In the interim, we did receive a concession from the laundry and bath people in that they've added a mid-day shower period for those of us who might want to exercise at lunch.

In the past two days we've begun to talk in specifics about the plans we are making for the transition period when the replacing CSH comes. We are preparing a presentation with lessons learned while on the deployment to keep them from making the same mistakes. We also plan to warn them against unrealistic expectations from the supply, transportation, or communication systems.

After hearing the planning phase timetable as coming from the administration side of our hospital, we've been joking that we are taking a process that should take two to three hours and "cramming" it into seven days. We all realize the upcoming process will be somewhat painful for us, but it means that our time here in the hospital will soon be ended.

11 Dec 03 – The temperature has turned colder in the past twenty-four hours, but the atmosphere has remained dry. The skies are cloudless and have been a shade of blue that is similar to a robin's egg. We continue to make preparations for the upcom-

ing Organizational Day. My soccer team – which had shown very poor overall attendance at our two prior games – showed up in force yesterday. Although our game was a dismal, losing effort, I think it demonstrated that many were looking forward to the soccer tournament on Saturday.

COL G. admitted an Iraqi mother and her daughter for rehabilitation care following a motor vehicle accident that happened to them at the end of October. The family lives in a village just outside our main gate and has been helpful when our physicians and medics have visited the village to immunize the children and treat any major illnesses. The two of them were initially treated at the Tikrit Teaching Hospital but were discharged recently, and the mother was not able to walk and care for her daughter or the other children in the family.

I have spent more and more time in the trailer in the past couple of days – even going there in the daytime to read a book. After all these months of being stuck in the Think Tank or elsewhere within the canvas walls of the hospital, it is nice to feel like I'm getting away. I have put some thoughts onto paper for the incoming physicians and will spend more time refining this guidance as it comes closer to time for us to turn over the duties.

Christmas is approaching, and I continue to pray for strength and wisdom to prepare my heart and mind for the separation from family and friends. I'm looking forward to the gifts that Ana has told me will start arriving in the coming days. She's hinted that the gifts will be themed around the Twelve Days of Christmas, and I'm excited about it. I am also feeling a certain amount of responsibility to maintain a solid attitude for those around me so as to witness about the importance of the season. I know that having the separation get me down would send the wrong message to those who might be watching my life.

14 Dec 03 – It has been several days since I've written, and the reasons for this are many. The biggest news here today is the capture of Saddam Hussein, which occurred last night in a small village 12 kilometers south of Tikrit. Earlier today we'd heard very high level security type rumors that he'd been captured and that a

more widespread announcement would be made later in the day. For us, the confirmation came when we saw the news conference from Baghdad today shortly after 1500. There were about twenty of us gathered around the TV in the DFAC, and our group included Salam and Nebo – our interpreters – and the Iraqi mother and daughter that are still under our care.

It came as no surprise that the three Iraqi adults were the ones with the largest smiles when Saddam's bearded image appeared on the screen. We all have a certain amount of giddiness right now that I'm finding hard to characterize. I don't think there'll be any immediate impact on our lives, but I do feel much more vindicated. I believe that history will shine favorably on the removal of this evil man from power. I'm honestly not at the point of being able to grasp the full significance of our participation here, but I trust that the years will build the experience in my memory and provide layers of appreciation for what we've done.

Today has been a relatively quiet day that included worship and Bible study this morning after getting the chance to sleep in a little and recover from all the athletic competition of the past two days. We held Organization Day yesterday under brilliant blue skies, and I think it was a great success. My soccer team only played in one game before being eliminated, but I enjoyed spending nearly the whole day outside watching others compete in various sporting events. We completed the day with a bonfire that provided a nice contrast of temperature for us as we huddled close to the heat while our backs were chilled by the winds that were blowing. Fortunately, my forty-one-year-old body is continuing to adjust to the increased level of exercise and activity that I'm asking of it. We started the morning in the thirty-degree weather with a three mile Fun Run in formation, complete with all the catchy cadences. The pace was slow enough that no one had to fall out, and I think that all who participated actually enjoyed it.

Though the commander arrived on Friday for her scheduled visit, I did not see her the whole weekend. Initially, I kept missing her in all the places she usually visits. By yesterday afternoon when

I began to realize that it might be possible to avoid her entirely, I decided to make a game of it and purposely stayed away.

15 Dec 03 – I received a nice box of cigars from my best friend, Nathan, which will enhance the mood of some of these cold nights. I also received a box of snacks and sweets sent by a women's Sunday school class from Oak Grove Baptist Church in my home-town of Boone. This church is the one that I grew up attending as a child, and the card that accompanied the box listed the names of the members of the class. As I read over the names of the mothers and female relatives of most of my childhood friends, thousands of memories came flooding back into my mind.

17 Dec 03 – It is morning, and I'm alone in the Think Tank because the surgeons are either sleeping or operating. The past two days have been busy for them. I don't know if the increase in number of trauma patients is directly attributable to the capture of Saddam or if it is related to normal offensive activities that were planned all along. In the end, the cause is somewhat irrelevant because the patients need care, and the reason for it is not important. I think that the approach of our Christmas holiday will be seen as a vulnerable time for us to the terrorists who are instigating the violence. I pray that there will be a respite for peace during Christmas, but that is probably a naïve desire.

The doctors are sponsoring another Open House in our area this coming Saturday evening to kick-off the Holiday season. While we want to foster an attitude of celebration, we are also looking for help in getting rid of most of the food items that we've accumulated over the past few weeks. Many of us are participating in a secret Santa gift exchange that will happen sometime soon. The musical play "I'll Be Home For Christmas" is being performed on Camp Speicher over three nights starting next week, and many of our hospital staff are involved with singing and speaking parts. Our hospital is sponsoring a 5K Jingle Bell Jog on Christmas morning, and the Chaplain is offering a Christmas mass on Christmas Eve and another service for the Protestants on Christmas Day. In total, I think we're doing a decent job of trying to fill our season with events that will both distract and satisfy.

23 Dec 03 – It's Tuesday afternoon, and I'm in the Think Tank writing the latest entry. Many days have passed since I last wrote, and not much has really happened lately. My daily routine now consists of awaking between 0600–0630 and stopping by the DFAC to grab some milk and cereal prior to coming in to the hospital, where I make coffee in the Think Tank. We also now have a refrigerator and small microwave that we use for food storage and preparation. As I eat breakfast, I usually connect to the Internet to read mail or talk with Ana. Then we have rounds at 0730, and these last around ten to fifteen minutes, depending on how many patients we have. On Monday, Wednesday, and Friday we have a staff meeting at 0800, which lasts around 30 minutes and centers on the discussion of keeping the hospital functioning from a multi-department standpoint. After morning report – or the staff meeting on certain days – I spend the next hour or so rounding on my patients and devising additional treatment plans or discharging them. By mid-morning, if there is no new patient consult for me to see, I settle in to do self-study in cardiology or reading for pleasure.

I've been trying to exercise at mid-day on most days unless there is a soccer game scheduled for later. Our soccer games start at 1500 each day and usually go until 1600. After the scheduled game there is usually a pick-up scrimmage game until the sun goes down around 1700. Then I come back into the hospital for afternoon rounds that are followed by dinner at 1730.

Three nights ago we held our Holiday Open House, and it was a huge success as our area was crowded with people for over an hour. We received many compliments and comments about our decorations, our Christmas lighting, and the spread of food. In the end, there was still food remaining, but we just scooped it up and took it out to the table in the PLX corridor and it was essentially gone by noon the next day.

Tonight is opening night of the musical "I'll Be Home For Christmas" that includes many cast members from our hospital. A group from all of Camp Speicher is producing it, and our contributors will be featured tonight and in the Christmas night performance. I am looking forward to the diversion, but I think they could have found another play with a different title. I plan to attend the Christmas night performance.

26 Dec 03 – As I sit here tonight to write this entry, I am content in the fact that I've survived being away from home and family at Christmas and actually managed to have a bit of enjoyment in small and isolated instances. It is certainly a Christmas that I'll never forget, and I'd venture to say that Ana and Noah and Logan and Caroline would agree. God has sustained me – yet again – and I never felt a hollowness of heart throughout the past two days. Our deployment family rallied together around one another and held each other up in the best ways we knew how, and we all made it through this challenge.

The remaining packages that Ana had mailed for me all arrived on the 24th, so I had the full complement of gifts that she'd planned for me. The day of the 24th was actually a busy clinical day for me because there were three new admissions for me to take care of. The air temperature was cold, but the sun was shining brightly throughout the day, and two teams were able to play an afternoon game of soccer while others played volleyball. I ran at midday but then worked for a while in the ER while Pam H. went to the PX for shopping.

At 2000 I attended a Protestant Christmas Eve service in the chapel, where we read several passages of Scripture, sang carols, listened to a short message from Chaplain K., and received Communion. Following the service, several of us were still in the mood to sing, so we embarked on an impromptu session of carol singing. We left the chapel and made our way through the ward, then the ICU, then throughout the rest of the hospital and administrative areas. Feeling that we were clearly on a roll, we then donned our coats and hats and gloves and ventured out into the night and wandered down into the LSA. Taking a cue from the practice everyone observes at Halloween, if we saw a light was on; we went to that trailer or tent to sing. Most of the members of our group were musically talented and more than made up for the rest of us – like me – who are better off blending their voices into a large group for concealment. Regardless of the talent level, we all genuinely enjoyed the adventure, and we were encouraged by many CSH members who also seemed to appreciate the experience.

At midnight I attended the Catholic Mass because it seemed like that most everyone else was going to attend, and I was curious. Due to the size of the crowd – which numbered more than sixty – the service was held in the DFAC and included some special music performed by the CSH members who usually provide choir music in our Sunday services. Then the priest from the 4th ID who has been leading the Thursday evening Bible study presided over the mass. At the close of the ceremony, they also partook of Communion, and we officially welcomed Christmas in Iraq. Afterward we invited all who were interested back to our physician's area because we again had put out desserts and light appetizers and coffee. We still had many food items left after our prior party, and some of us had already received more in the mail. The attendance was good, and most of the items were finished before the group dwindled at around 0200. We left everything out on the tables and retired for what was planned to be an early morning.

We slept a little late but still awoke by 0730 on Christmas morning and gathered to participate in the Jingle Bell Jog. The distance was a manageable 5K, and many people came dressed in festive garments as had been suggested by the flyers. There were several Santa hats and elves' ears, and two of the nurses had wrapped themselves in wrapping paper and were wearing brightly colored stockings. The weather cooperated, the sky was a brilliant blue color, and the thirty-eight degree air temperature added a distinctive crispness to our celebration. We all finished the run by the thirty-minute mark – the faster runners completed the course in less than twenty minutes – and then moved to the DFAC for the presentation of awards and door prizes. Afterward we hit the showers, and I came into the hospital to see the patients I was caring for. Two of them had improved significantly, and I was able to discharge them. The other two patients settled in to enjoy their Christmas in the CSH.

Shortly after noon I joined a five-ton truck full of other soldiers to go to the prepared Christmas meal at the main DFAC, where we'd gone on Thanksgiving. Instead of walking right in like the last time, we waited about 30 minutes to join the serving line. Our wait was rewarded with several choices of meat entrées, including turkey and ham, along with several vegetables. Completing the meal was fresh garden salad, shrimp cocktail, and assorted pies and cakes for dessert.

After coming back to the CSH, I relaxed for a while and then went to the MWR tent at 1500 to participate in the secret Santa gift exchange. I gave Chaplain K. a coffee mug, some coffee, a Christian music CD, and some chocolate treats. The gift was amusing because the cup was one I bought at the local PX, and the caption read "Happiness is Iraq in my rearview mirror." The chaplain had previously mentioned several times that he thought it was a tacky cup. Unfortunately, I'd already bought the gift for him, and when he saw the gift he thought it was hilarious. I received a Dale Earnhardt Jr. coffee mug from my secret Santa, who was my racing buddy, Marco O., our pharmacist.

My wife and family members are truly generous, and it always shows in the gifts that I receive. The highlights of my gifts were craft items that Noah, Logan, and Caroline made and decorated. There's no getting around the idea that I'd have given virtually anything to be able to be home with my family, watching as they open their gifts while I open mine and just spend the time together with them. But I experienced a great deal of peace in my heart that comforted me in spite of not being with my family, and I give thanks to God for providing me with that feeling.

Later in the evening, I crawled again into the back of a five-ton and joined the group as we rode over to the other side of Camp Speicher to see our CSH members participate in the production of "I'll Be Home For Christmas." The performance turned out to be a real treat, as they all did a wonderful job of bringing the story to over 100 people in the audience. Some of our fellow soldiers have real acting and singing talent, and it was nice to see that other manifestation of their personalities.

After returning from the show, I was able to get online with Ana and the kids for a short time before we experienced technical difficulties with our connection that cut our time short. At around

2200 several of the senior officers who are all physicians and nurses retired down to the LSA for some food and cigars. We all concluded our evening under clear and cold skies at around 2400 by hugging each other and thanking one another for the support that had allowed us all to survive Christmas away from home.

15 / Planning for the Transfer of Authority

31 Dec 03 – It's Wednesday morning – the last day of the year – and as I write to catch up on the events of the past few days, I'm mindful of the events that have occurred to shape the year 2003 into one that I'll never forget. From this day forward, I'll say that 2003 was the year that I "joined" the Army. I had never really been integrated into the full Army lifestyle of wearing the uniform all day every day or being deployed in the field environment and getting used to field sanitation issues, MRE's, "battle rattle," and narrow cots. It's been a year of denial of self – both spiritually and physically – and learning about the sacrifice that it takes to serve in the military and not see your family and friends for months at a time.

I was fortunate to be able to go home at the eight month mark for the medical conference, but most soldiers here are now in the 10th month of not seeing their loved ones. It's been a year of learning what it means to go to war and to face difficult issues in your life about maintaining the love of Christ in your heart toward a people who want to kill your fellow soldiers at every opportunity they get. It's been a year to relearn the concept of depending on God to sustain through all the challenges because "For when I am weak, then I am strong" (2 Corinthians 12:10, NIV). It's been a year of falling in love again with my wife for the strength of character that she's shown through our separation and under the weight of the added responsibilities that she has with being, in essence, a single mother. It's been a year of missing my children so badly that it literally hurts. It's been a year that I'll never forget.

03 Jan 04 – This is my first entry of the New Year, and it's a calm, foggy Saturday morning. The power is off in the Think Tank

as a result of the once weekly shutdown of generators for routine maintenance. It should only be down for about 30 minutes. During the hot months of the summer, the time when the power was off passed interminably slow, but now it doesn't seem like such a big deal. After a busy week leading up to New Year's Day, our inpatient census has steadily declined. I discharged my only patient earlier this morning.

On New Year's Eve we held a party in the PLX corridor starting around 2100 and going until after midnight. The decorations consisted of Christmas lights, balloons, and banners. We also filled several tables with food, and I learned that the physicians are not the only ones who had extra items that needed to be put out for consumption. We passed the time with games – Pictionary, Twister, Spades, a limbo contest – and conversation. At midnight we had a surrogate dropping of the ball. Diane S. had an inflatable globe of the world, which we tied with cord around one of the suspended lights, and starting at T-30 seconds, we all did the countdown aloud while Diane lowered the globe to the floor. It was hilarious, and we all loved it and felt at that moment that Times Square had nothing on us. At midnight – by an arbitrarily selected watch – we all hugged and celebrated making it past another milestone on our journey together.

New Year's Day passed without incident or much fanfare. Special meals were offered at the main DFAC's, but our DFAC also served traditional meal items like greens and black-eyed peas. I don't think many people rode the trucks over like they had on Thanksgiving and Christmas. Many people gathered around the TV's when the football games started later in the day, but otherwise, it was a laid-back celebration.

We're slowly making ready for the redeployment by sorting through our possessions and deciding what to mail, what to carry, what to pack into the footlockers, and so forth. Even though we don't have a firm date, we all know the time is getting short, and while the end of the tunnel may not be in view yet, at least most of us feel like we've finally entered the tunnel.

10 Jan 04 – I currently have no patients, and there are only

three patients total in the hospital right now. Rob D. returned yesterday from a trip to Ibn Sina to deliver a lecture on prostate cancer to the Iraqi Medical Society and to visit our main element in Baghdad. His lecture was well received, and he said he fielded many questions from the audience that demonstrated they were reviewing current literature. We haven't heard this addressed specifically, but I believe it's because the Internet is now available when it hadn't been before. Based on what our interpreter Salam has told us, the Internet was closely guarded and essentially restricted to a select few and only for official government use. Since the fall of the regime, Internet cafés have been springing up all around, and there are no restrictions on its use. Rob reported that his impressions were similar to what we've all found when we visited Ibn Sina. There is considerably more drama surrounding the practice of healthcare there, although we can't identify a justifiable reason why that would be so. The number of trauma cases is higher than here, but they also have more resources there to deal with the workload.

The biggest news coming from there is that their replacements are apparently in theatre now and are expected within the next few days to begin the TOA (transfer of authority). The TOA is happening a bit sooner than what we'd been told to expect, and I think that has good implications for us as well. Given that their TOA has been accelerated, we believe that our replacements will follow soon after theirs.

13 Jan 04 – Two days ago was Sunday, and we had a pleasant worship service and Bible study afterward. We're excited that we potentially have less than four more services to meet together, and though we'll miss each other's fellowship, we're all anxious to return to our home congregations again. Our clinical load remains rather light, as we've averaged only four to eight patients over the past few days. The weather had been nice and cooperative for us until late last night, when we were treated to a thunderous show, complete with lights and sounds. Then it began to rain. And it rained. And then it rained some more. And then it really began to pour. We awoke to puddles everywhere, and our lovely soccer field was submerged under inches of water and will likely not host any more games the

rest of this week. Today I heard many people speak about how the storm kept them awake, but I slept as soundly as I have in weeks. I heard the chaplain joking today about having dreams of "two by two" last night.

15 Jan 04 – It's Thursday morning, and I just finished putting my foot locker and secondary duffel bag in a milvan that is being loaded and sent in two days toward Ft Bragg. It should arrive within a month after we return. I've been able to condense my possessions into the things I packed today, plus my rucksack, my primary duffel bag, and another footlocker that will be used to transport my professional equipment like books and the portable echocardiogram machine. Most of the other soldiers have had to mail at least one package home to be able to fit their remaining items in the allotted bags.

Yesterday we treated an interesting patient who'd sustained a gunshot wound to his chest. He was wearing his flak vest with a self-made plate of steel that wasn't provided with the vest. The steel plate was effective at stopping the bullet such that it barely pierced the skin over his left breast and caused a laceration less than an inch long. He is sore and will have some bruising, but is obviously blessed to be alive. I admitted him for overnight observation to be certain that there were no cardiac abnormalities, and he did well. Prior to his discharge I snapped a couple of pictures of him with his injury and the steel plate.

18 Jan 04 – This morning I joined over a dozen other runners from the CSH as we participated in the "Terror De Tikrit," a ten kilometer run sponsored on Camp Speicher by the 4th Aviation Brigade. It was advertised as "the most dangerous 10K poker race you'll ever run." It was called a poker race because we collected playing cards along the route – they used the famous Most Wanted cards of Iraqi targets – and at the end we played a hand of poker to qualify for additional prizes. My hand was three of a kind, but that couldn't compete with another member of our group who collected five of a kind – obviously because of the multiple decks. He went on to win the overall prize, which was a gift certificate for three days and two nights donated by the Stardust Casino in Las Vegas.

During the race things really became muddy as we left the pavement and ran along a cross-country type course that took us over the top of two ammunition bunkers that rose up out of the ground at least fifteen to twenty feet. The path then led us through bombed out buildings and weaving around several partially destroyed Iraqi fighter planes. The final turn for the finish line brought us over several areas of ruts and mud puddles before finishing on gravel in front of the main DFAC in the aviation area. In all, it was a fun experience, and I'm just happy and satisfied to finish because I believe that is the longest distance I've ever run. My time was a respectable fifty-six minutes, and I couldn't believe how fresh I felt at the end.

21 Jan 04 – On Monday I was a bit sore from the 10K run on Sunday, but not as bad as what I'd expected. Yesterday I shot some baskets for a while to loosen up and then went for a short run, and it all felt pretty good. We've had to cancel our soccer games again so far this week because our field is still muddy from all the rains.

I spoke to Bill on the phone today, and he told me that their replacements are in the midst of orientation lectures and briefings and haven't ventured into the clinical arena yet. At present, they plan to hand over the clinical duties to them this coming Monday, the twenty-sixth. He said that the replacements – about two hundred and fifty of them – are living in a warehouse near the hospital that is without electricity or climate control and their latrines are somewhat remote as well. He went on to say that there were some sad looking faces among the people he'd met so far.

24 Jan 04 – It's Saturday, and today is Noah's eighth birthday. It is middle of the day there, and I know from a conversation with Ana two days ago that they're at an Upward Basketball game right now, so I plan to call him in about an hour or so. I ordered him a jersey that features Dale Earnhardt Jr., which I think is appropriate since he's my favorite driver, and his car number is eight, which corresponds with Noah's age. This is the second time that I'm missing one of my children's birthdays, and I haven't gotten any better at accepting it.

The big story around here the past few days has been the lack of patients and the sorry weather. Fortunately, the two appear linked, and we're all thankful that we haven't been faced with trying to accomplish numerous medevacs in the recent weather.

Two days ago, John K. invited me to accompany him on a walk out toward the periphery of Camp Speicher to visit an abandoned bunker. John has been making this walk for weeks, and he had invited me often. On Thursday I found it too windy to really run, and the moisture on our soccer field guaranteed that our games were cancelled for the whole week. The sky was overcast, and the wind was beginning to really gust, but we made our way along paths worn into the grass at the end of the runway toward the north. In the far distance, I could barely see our target as it rose up from the flat surroundings.

As we walked, I asked John to give me a condensed version of church history as he understood and remembered it. I asked questions when I needed clarification, but for the most part, John talked and did a great job of weaving Bible history of the early Christian church with the geographical and political influences that shaped how the major religions of the Christian faith came about. I was so inspired by the conversation that I made a mental note to seek out a good written history to find and read when I get home. I've always enjoyed history as a topic as long as I could choose the topic and approach it on my own terms. I find that to be very true now, and it's been inspired in no small part by our being here in this region of the world, where history as we know it originated.

It's later in the evening now, and I just spoke to Noah on the satellite phone. He's had a good birthday so far, and several sets of families that we know from church are there now to celebrate with him. He scored three baskets this morning in his basketball game and sounded thrilled about it. Of course, those are the first points he's ever scored in competition, and even though it seems trivial, I'm more than a little disappointed that I wasn't there. I don't like the Army very much right now.

26 Jan 04 – I got an e-mail from Bill today that indicated they were ready to hand off the clinical duties to the portion of the 31st CSH from Ft Bliss, Texas, that is replacing them. He says that he's

now spending a lot of time reading, sleeping, and going to the gym near the hospital. It's funny how we've come full circle to the way it was when we first arrived in theatre last March before the war began. I think that we'll also ease into that kind of existence again once our replacements are here. He still didn't say when they might be leaving Baghdad, and I think it's because the details are still being arranged.

Yesterday was Sunday and it was a pleasant day of weather here. The sunshine was a welcome relief and it elevated our spirits somewhat. We especially needed our spirits lifted because two nights ago a US soldier was brought in late at night after being injured in an explosion. He had sustained a large soft-tissue wound through his right flank that had destroyed much of his intestines, side muscles, pelvis, and kidney. The surgeons operated on him for several hours in an attempt to gain control of the massive bleeding, but their efforts were ultimately futile. Thankfully, there have been no other major traumas of late.

The sick call area is still busy, but hardly any of them have diagnoses that require admission, and many of them are bogus complaints of musculoskeletal pain. Several of the units on post are planning a physical fitness test in the coming weeks and the soldiers are looking to avoid having to take the test. Fortunately, Diane S. and Teresa H. can usually see through their fabricated symptoms and discharge them with a decent scolding for trying to abuse the system.

Yesterday John K. gave a great message about knowing God's will in our lives, and then we had a moving communion experience together. Sherman C. presided over the communion portion of our service, and he spoke some touching words about our congregation and how we've grown over the months together. He pointed out what a multi-cultural group we are, with most Christian denominations being represented, and how we'd likely never be in the same kind of congregation ever again in our lives. He reminded us how we've grown as individuals and as members of the group, and he praised us for the love we've shown one another and the way in which we've demonstrated the love of Christ one to another. The fifteen of us present, who really represent the core group of our congregation, passed around the bread and the cup and shared them with one another. And then, as it says in Scripture, we sang a hymn and were dismissed.

In reflection, everything Sherman said was true. It has been an amazing spiritual experience, and it has been enhanced by the fellow believers here in the hospital such as Colin G, our commander, and Joy W., the chief nurse in the ICU, who's led the music, and John K., our chaplain, and Sherman. It's a major part of this deployment that I'll never forget.

28 Jan 04 – Today will be forever historic in the grand scheme of the deployment of the 28th CSH for OIF because the 67th CSH main body arrived to replace us. The small advance party had come two days ago but didn't include any physicians. The main body is about one hundred and twenty strong, and they seem genuinely pleased to be here from what limited interaction I've had with them so far. I'm sure that much of that emotion is similar to when we completed our long convoy through Iraq during the early stages of the war and had arrived at Dogwood to set up the original hospital. After traveling, it just feels so good and rewarding to settle somewhere and begin doing what you're trained to do.

On the clinical side, they have a different line-up of providers compared to us. They have only four physicians for this location: one general surgeon, one orthopedist, one internist, and one emergency physician. They apparently also have an adult nurse practitioner who would be analogous to Diane and Teresa, but who isn't planning on working as an independent provider for the sick call mission. That is one area that they'll need to address after we're gone because Diane and Teresa routinely see between 30 and 40 patients a day in our sick call area, and those patients won't just stop coming because we're not here.

The weather has been pleasant enough – no more rain or gusting winds – and we christened a new soccer field yesterday afternoon with a couple of hours of scrimmage. We were able to find a flat and grassy area out behind the laundry and bath tent and moved the goals over to that space. The new field has real grass – although sparse – and subtle ridges in certain areas that seem to give it character. For the short time that we have remaining, it should more than suit our needs. Our league has, for the most part, been dissolved because of the increased number of briefings and meetings that are happening during the TOA. We've decided that from this point forward we'll just play pick-up games amongst whoever comes and is not involved in the briefings.

I waited in line fifteen minutes tonight to get my food at the DFAC, and I remarked that is the first time I've had to wait this long since we were crowded in Camp Victory last March. I realize that the lines for food, for showers, and for the laundry services will be significantly increased now because we've doubled in size. I don't think any of us in the 28th will complain too much because we realize that it is a short-term inconvenience, and it has only developed because our replacements are here.

01 Feb 04 – It is Sunday here, and it's been several days since I've written. Our workload has remained relatively low, but we've been involved in the TOA with the members of the 67th CSH. On the whole, they are a nice group and seem eager to learn from our experiences and begin the work that they've come here to do. The days have been filled with what seems to me like an endless number of briefings and introductory sessions. Bill told me last week that they were "wearing out" the members of the 31st CSH with lectures and briefings there in Baghdad, and I'm seeing that phenomenon firsthand now. I'd certainly shorten the duration of the sessions they're going through by at least fifty percent and ease them into taking over our roles far sooner than our TOA calls for.

We are in the fifth day, and today is the first day that they're supposed to be working a half-day in the so-called left seat or driver's position while we supervise in the right seat. For physicians, I think this concept is insulting, but the whole TOA process is less for the physicians than it is for the other workers. My counterpart, Bobby J., has already started admitting and following some of the medicine patients who need hospitalization. Today he went with COL G. on a convoy downtown to the teaching hospital, and tomorrow he plans to spend his first day working in the ACC seeing sick-call patients.

According to the schedule, we are to relinquish all clinical duties to the 67th CSH tomorrow, and there is a MASCAL exercise planned for late morning. That will be the final clinical instruction that we take part in, and from that point they are technically on their own. Of course, it looks like we'll still be around for a few more days and will be available to answer any questions that might arise or pitch in for specialty needs – such as if a patient comes in that needs a cardiology consult – but for the most part, our clinical responsibility ends tomorrow.

Two nights ago we held another open house in the Think Tank to meet as many of the new hospital members as possible and to continue to get rid of our collection of food. The turnout was pretty light by our prior standards, but the group that came was a nice collection of officers and enlisted, and we got to know them better than we would have otherwise. Last night there was a party in the PLX corridor that initially drew a larger crowd of 67th folks but was prematurely terminated around 2100 when Camp Speicher came under mortar attack for the first time in over two months. Ironically, I'd just talked two days ago to the groups that I was touring about how safe Camp Speicher was and that it hadn't been attacked in quite a while. Although the rounds landed at least a mile away from us, we heard the explosion and were instructed to don our flack vests and Kevlar helmets and report to the bunkers in our LSA. We waited there for about forty-five minutes until the all clear was given and then just stayed down there.

Over the past few evenings, there is a small group of us that has started gathering together to reminisce and dream about our redeployment process. The group includes me, Rob, Teresa H., Diane S., Ann H. and Michelle R. The last four are all nurses in leadership positions. Last night, we congregated again outside mine and Rob's trailer. We had a hilarious discussion of past prom experiences, and we realized from our year of graduation that we were all basically the same age, except Michelle. These are definitely good people and I've built great deployment friendships with them. I'll always treasure the experience, but it's now time to go home more than ever.

I slept in late this morning until around 0800 (as has become the custom on Sunday mornings) and then attended what should be our last worship service in Tikrit. Several members of the 67th joined our usual crowd today and John preached a good sermon from Ephesians 6 about putting on the armor of Christ and how closely that mirrored our need to put on all our military protective gear to remain safe in the world.

03 Feb 04 – I awoke just before 0300 and hurriedly got dressed and went over to the MWR tent to watch the Super Bowl. After entering, I realized that the whole MWR tent was in the low-lying area of the LSA, and it was literally flooded. Despite the soggy conditions, around twenty-five people had gathered to watch the game and cheer for the teams. It was a more subdued crowd than I think it would have been if the weather had been good and our feet weren't partially submerged in water. Nonetheless, everyone seemed to enjoy the broadcast, and I can now report that I've watched the Super Bowl in a foreign land at an unreasonable time of morning during a war.

Knowing that I had no clinical duties, I slept in a little later today and came to the hospital around 0800. With nothing official to be done, I spent time on the Internet and then watched a movie and then read. In the afternoon, I went down to the LSA to begin to organize what's left of my gear for packing. We learned today that we'd load our duffel bags onto the trucks tomorrow morning between 0900 and 1200. Our destination is Camp Anaconda in Balad, where the 21st CSH had been located and now the second half of the 31st CSH is located.

This afternoon we were called to a formation on the basketball court and participated in a combat patch ceremony. During the course of the ceremony, we learned about the history of the 28th CSH in prior campaigns and the significance of the unit patches that all soldiers wear on their left sleeves. After serving in combat, a soldier is then authorized to wear that unit patch on their right shoulder for the remainder of their career. At the end of the ceremony today, we were given 44th Medical Command patches to have sewn on our uniforms. Several of us then sealed the event with a celebratory cigar as we watched the sun go down. I silently remarked to myself that if all goes well, we'd only see that occur two more times in Iraq.

04 Feb 04 – After packing my duffel this morning, I went to the PX for one last visit to see if there were any meaningful souvenirs that I hadn't seen. I found a couple of small stuffed camels for the kids with the word Iraq imprinted on the side. I bought Ana the nicest Operation Iraqi Freedom t-shirt that I could find, but of course, I realize I'm opening myself up to the syndrome of "my husband was away for a whole year in a war-zone and all I got was this lousy t-shirt.

It's later in the evening now, and I've just returned from a short prayer time in which John K. led us in prayer and read Psalm 91 to encourage us as we prepare for tomorrow's ground convoy to Balad. Many people prayed and gave thanks to God for the challenges and triumphs we'd experienced during this past year. We were speaking of the group as a whole, but I know that most of us realized that everything we experienced as a group had also translated into changes in our lives on a personal level. I think we were all feeling the need to vocalize those changes and give credit to God. As we broke up the meeting, we sensed that something special had happened to our small group of committed believers, and it was unlikely that we'd ever have an experience like this again. It was bittersweet, but we knew that it meant we'd be going home.

16 / Leaving Iraq

08 Feb 04 – Four days ago I slept anxiously through my last night in Tikrit. I awoke early and was able to get on the Internet one last time the morning of the 5th and chat with Ana. It was the first time in over a week that we'd communicated on the computer, and she quickly brought me up to speed about her trip to Disney with the kids. Then I hurried down to the trailer for one last time and finished loading my rucksack onto our five-ton truck. After what seemed like one more roll call than we actually needed, the command was given to load up the trucks. Shortly after 0900 our convoy of fifteen trucks left the compound of our hospital on Camp Speicher, and we all cheered with great enthusiasm. Several members of the 67th CSH were outside holding an American flag and gave us a farewell salute as we left.

The weather was cool but clear, and this was important because we were in the back of 5-ton trucks that were uncovered, and we were exposed to the elements. In preparation for the convoy, the enlisted soldiers had placed sandbags on the floor of the trucks, and we sat on assorted pads on the sandbags in the center of the truck facing outward to afford us a better view of any enemy activity. Fortunately, the trip was uneventful, and we arrived in Balad at Camp Anaconda just before noon. We spent the next few hours getting settled into a temporary area that they call 'tent city' because it is in an unfinished area of the camp, and with the recent rains, it had also flooded and was by now a virtual quagmire of mud. What little gravel that was present wasn't enough to compensate for the mud. It was as bad as any place we'd been. The tents had a cement slab for a floor but were unheated and damp.

After navigating the mud to reach the DFAC for dinner, several of us enjoyed our last cigar in Iraq before retiring for bed. After the stress of traveling in the convoy and dealing with the mud, I was tired and promptly fell asleep around 2100. I awoke in the middle of the night to the sound of more rain, but quickly rolled over and slept again.

By the next morning the rain had stopped, and since the mud was so bad to begin with, I don't think the rain had any noticeable impact. After a breakfast of power bars – because I didn't want to venture through the mud again to reach the DFAC – I finished my packing for our afternoon flight. In standard fashion, we were required to arrive at the passenger terminal of the airfield four hours before the flight. By 1400 we'd gone through the cursory customs station and were loaded into the final "sterile" area that we were not allowed to leave until our flight. Within the hour, we were instructed to grab our gear and follow our guide onto the flight line, where we walked up the ramp onto the back of the C-130 that would take us out of the country. Shortly after 1505 on 06 Feb 04, the wheels of our flight lifted off from the airfield at Balad to bring us out of Iraq. An immediate cheer went up from nearly everyone on the flight. After a tactical take-off that included several heavily banked turns, we climbed to altitude and settled in for the ninety-minute flight south to Kuwait.

Around 1630 we gently touched down at Ali Al-Salem Airfield in western Kuwait. When the rest of our group had arrived safely – around 1900 – we then loaded all our rucks and duffels onto the back of transport trucks and climbed onto five large and comfortable buses for our ninety minute ride to Camp Arifjan, which is south of Kuwait City. It was a striking contrast to the initial bus rides we experienced last March when we arrived. We were now relaxed, un-crowded, unencumbered by all the protective gear, and able to ride with the curtains open on the bus and not feel hidden and claustrophobic.

We arrived at Arifjan and were reunited with the main body of our CSH. After unloading our gear, we moved onto the empty cots within the large warehouse. Like I'd said on an earlier entry, I think there is symmetry to us finishing our tour in a warehouse. The difference this time is that the warehouse itself is much larger and can hold us all together, and our mood is drastically improved from last March when we were at Camp Doha. After quick greetings to those who were still awake, some of our group went to eat at the midnight chow, some went to use the phones, some went to shower, and others, like me, just went to sleep.

Yesterday morning, I slept in a bit but awoke in time to go to breakfast at the DFAC. It wasn't as nice as the one at Camp Doha in terms of food selection, but it's more spacious, is nicely decorated, and has a large projection TV along the main wall. After breakfast, we began having formations and continued to have them throughout the day to disseminate information and to coordinate our activities. In the afternoon, we went over to a large compound that contains milvans, including the one we'd packed with our gear in Tikrit several weeks ago. I was under the impression that it'd left Tikrit and was being shipped on boats and would arrive sometime around when we did. But yesterday afternoon, we had to unpack our footlockers and duffel bags and lay all the items on the ground for inspection by the MP's. Fortunately, I didn't possess anything that was illegal to bring home, but many of the soldiers did not fare as well.

Near the DFAC are a PX, a gym, an MWR tent with large-screen TV's, an Internet café, and several fast-food restaurants such as Subway, Burger King, and Baskin-Robbins. Later in the evening, after dinner, someone remarked that the whole area almost has the feel of a county fair because of the sights, sounds, and smells. When everything settled down, Bill and I set up a movie to watch, and it attracted several of the doctors and we spent the evening laughing. This morning I awoke before 0600 and went over to the Internet café and was able to get online for a session of instant messaging with Ana.

We chatted for about 30 minutes, and Noah even typed messages to me for a while. He told me that it was hard waiting for me to come home and that he missed me very much. It's a good thing that he couldn't see me shedding tears. He was very excited because he'd scored again in his basketball game that morning and had lost another baby tooth. I assured him that it wouldn't be long until I was home. Given that it was such a beautiful morning – cool with a brilliant clear blue sky – I decided to go for a run and took off to explore more of the installation. After a good run and a luke-warm shower – the facilities here leave a great deal to be desired in terms of water that is definitely not hot and comes out in a weak stream – I joined Bill and the others for lunch at the DFAC. Since lunch we've just been relaxing in the warehouse and looking for-ward to dinner.

From my run this morning, I saw that there are several perma-nent buildings on the other side of the facility, for use by the people who are assigned here for a full one-year rotation. I can tell that we've already slipped back into the same mindset that we had at Camp Doha last year. Our biggest challenge is to fill the day with scattered activities so as to combat the boredom that is inherent in waiting. The major difference – in our favor – is that the wait this time is for our ride home, and I can tell that everyone's attitude is a bit more tolerant and patient than it was last year.

We're scheduled to fly from the main military airport in Kuwait City on commercial-style jets in two lifts on 13 and 14 February. The first lift is the smaller one, and has room for only 131 pas-sengers. The second one would bring the remaining 300 soldiers. Once the flights are confirmed and we're within twenty-four hours of departure, we have to go through the inspection process again with our rucksack and the other duffel bag. At that point, I'll really begin to get excited.

The integration of the two segments of the CSH back into one has been relatively painless from the physician standpoint. It has been easy to hang out again with the friends I had when we first deployed. There are so many new faces now that many people spend their time walking around in the warehouse trying to remember if that person they just passed is someone they've forgotten or they are new since we were all together last June. Regardless, the commander has made good on her promise that we'd all go home together.

11 Feb 04 – It is Wednesday afternoon, and I'm sitting in my folding chair beside my cot in the warehouse. I hadn't carried any of

my chairs down here from Tikrit, but knowing that we'd be doing a lot of sitting, Rob and I bought two chairs from the PX here last Saturday for eight dollars. They've already been worth the price to avoid having to slump over on the cot each day. There has been only one formation today for accountability. The temperature is comfortable, with cool nights and manageable highs in the afternoons. It also helps that we're able to stay in our PT uniform throughout the day if we choose. When the wind gusts it blows the sand around. We are all having some flashbacks to our days in Dogwood, but so far, there has not been a shamal.

Our activities over the past three days have been quite repetitive. I visit the Internet café before breakfast and then come back to the warehouse after breakfast for our short formation. Then we spend the day exercising, reading, and napping. I've also done some shopping in the past two days. I found a t-shirt for each of the kids and found a nice handmade Indian rug. After soliciting advice from several friends here and Ana via the phone and Internet, I found one that I think will look nice in our dining room. I believe it was a good deal for the quality, and I took it next door from the rug shop to the post office and packaged it for mailing home.

Yesterday the manifest list for the first flight was announced. It includes the names of 80 plus soldiers who came late to the CSH as replacements and did their initial deployment in processing through Ft Bliss in El Paso, Texas. That group is being allowed to go first because they need to make it to Ft Bliss by Monday evening of next week to begin their redeployment out-processing there. Other names on the first flight are people who didn't leave the theatre for any reason such as leave, TDY, or transports since we arrived last March.

As of now, the first flight is still scheduled to leave from the airport in Kuwait City at 1200 on the 13th and arrive back at Ft Bragg later in the evening of that same day with the allowances made for travel time and time-zone differences. The majority of us are on the second flight that is scheduled to leave here around 1900 on the 14th and should arrive around 0500 on the morning of the 15th.

We're told that the only thing that would disrupt this schedule now would be mechanical problems or severe weather.

14 Feb 04 – It's Valentine's Day here, and the schedule for our departure has been fairly accurate to this point. Yesterday morning, the first group was a bit behind schedule but still left, and they haven't returned from the airport because of not being able to get on the flight. They had done their customs inspection layout the prior afternoon and then loaded their duffel bags into the truck afterwards. They were allowed to keep their rucksacks out and packed them to take along early yesterday morning. As of now, we're hearing that they won't arrive at Pope until around 0200 on the 14th.

We awoke early this morning so that we could do our last minute chores and eat breakfast prior to having our customs inspection at 0700. We were able to lay out all our items from the rucksacks and duffel bags, and when finished, we loaded all that baggage onto the trucks. After loading our gear onto the trucks, we only waited another couple of hours, and then boarded the buses for our ride to the airport. We sat on the buses for almost an hour while "last minute" issues were resolved, but the mood was surprisingly tolerant, and I'm sure it's because we all realized that we were getting closer with each step to leaving.

Around 1100 we departed Camp Arifjan to muted cheers and began our ninety-minute ride to the airport in Kuwait City. In spite of our bus driver being fairly incompetent, we arrived in one piece and unloaded from the bus to begin our processing at the airport. Over the next couple of hours, we were subjected to customs forms and briefings and a final customs inspection that was more hype than substance, in my experience. We waited less than an hour in the sterile area before being given the instructions to grab our gear and move out to load the buses. At this point, everyone was holding only their weapons and their carry-on bags. It was a distinct contrast to the way we'd arrived in theatre twelve months prior with our entire "battle rattle."

The buses dropped us beside our transportation home – a large United 747 airplane. When I reached the top of the stairs and entered the plane, the first sergeant directed me to the left side that led to the business class seats. It was the first time in many months that I'd received any special privileges on the basis of my rank. I was in no mood to feel guilty for this distinction and happily settled into the oversized seat in the more spacious section. Further forward, the commander and other "specially selected" individuals were settled into the first class section. I could not easily discern the criteria used for that group, but I wasn't looking to quibble given my location in the plane relative to the majority of our traveling party. After some delays on the ground while more "last-minute issues" were resolved, our flight began to roll shortly after 1915 local time – only fifteen minutes behind schedule. Needless to say, the crew of the flight was treated to the first of several cheers when the wheels finally lifted off from Kuwaiti soil.

17 / Home again

16 Feb 04 – We're home, we're home, we're home! After taking off from Kuwait, we flew for several hours and landed in Prague for a two-hour layover for refueling. During the layover we were allowed to deplane and relax in a sequestered terminal, so I can't say that I know any more about the city than I did before. From Prague we flew for nine hours and landed directly at Pope Air Force Base, adjacent to Ft Bragg. During the flight, the United Airlines crew was extremely accommodating to us, and we enjoyed several in-flight movies and multiple meals. On more than one occasion, they unanimously expressed their appreciation to us for the job that we had done and seemed genuinely proud to be accompanying us back to the United States. It was a touching attitude. The second of our group cheers arose sometime late in the flight when the pilot informed us that we had crossed into US airspace.

The third group cheer – and loudest one – erupted when we felt the wheels touch down in North Carolina shortly after 0400 local time. As we taxied to the familiar position on the tarmac outside of Green Ramp, I spent the time reflecting back over the year and the experiences we'd had. In my mind, I couldn't decide between the emotions of elation or relief. In the end, I was just glad to be home. After several minutes the doors opened, and we deplaned down the long staircase to a greeting party at the foot of the steps that included the commanding general of the 44th Medical Command, the commander of Womack Army Medical Center and the Command Sergeant Major of the 44th. After shaking their hands and accepting their words of welcome, I veered out of line and did what I'd promised myself I'd do – bend over and kiss the ground.

Standing on US soil was an amazing feeling. As we deplaned,

we formed up over to the side of the plane and waited for everyone to unload. As we stood there we could see the open doors of Green Ramp one hundred yards ahead of us, and we could hear the low roar that was coming from our families and friends as they patiently waited there.

After what seemed like an eternity to me, the entire group of 317 was finally in formation, and we began a slow march toward the open doors. Green Ramp has a series of large garage-type doors, and the one on the far right end was the only one open. From my position near the head of our column, I could see many people packed around the opening with signs and balloons and waving arms. As we approached, I also noticed the lights of a camera crew from a local TV station that was there to cover our arrival, and I heard the sounds of a band playing patriotic music. From the outside, however, I could not have anticipated the pageantry that awaited us when we finally moved through the open doorway and turned left to fill our columns into the far left of the building. It literally took my breath away and was more than I had anticipated, although, in retrospect, I guess I shouldn't have been so surprised by our welcome.

The tears were already running down my cheeks before we entered the building, but they intensified even more when we were finally all inside and the band began to play The National Anthem as we were brought to the position of attention while facing our families. My emotions were strong, and I didn't try to hold back the sense of relief that I felt about being home. Fortunately, the greeting remarks were kept short, and we were quickly released to join our families. The only negative aspect for me was that I was located at the far left of the formation in the building, and it took me several minutes to find Ana and the kids and to see the sign that they were holding for me. While I searched, I was treated to innumerable reunions amongst the soldiers and family members who were there to welcome us home.

Eventually I found my family amid the happy confusion, and we shared several moments of hugs and tears. It was clearly the best I'd felt in months, and I was so relieved to be holding on to each of them. While we visited with each other, we made hasty introductions of our friends and their family members. Soon our leaders were telling us that we needed to separate from family and board the buses that waited outside to take us back over to the company area to turn in our weapons and receive an initial briefing on our schedule for the coming days.

Bill's wife Shannon and Ana had pre-positioned my truck at the company area the day before. After we loaded on the buses they went back to our house to let the kids sleep a little before we arrived back home. They had gotten the kids up at around 0200 and gone by the Krispy-Kreme doughnut shop for us. The kids had behaved very well but needed a little more sleep to help them prepare for the long day ahead. It was Caroline's birthday that day, and there was a party already planned for her later in the afternoon.

After we rode the buses back, we received our initial briefings, turned in our weapons for the last time, and were released to go home around 0830. Because it was the midst of a four-day weekend, we were released until a morning formation on Tuesday the 17th. Driving was a bit strange, but Bill and I made it back to my house without incident and settled into the process of integrating ourselves back into the civilized world and the lives of our families.

This is the first opportunity that I've taken to write since arriving home, and the whole situation is still somewhat surreal to me. A full year of my life has passed since I've been away, and while there are so many things that are different, in other areas, I feel like that I was never gone. I look forward to the challenges of becoming an integral part of my family again and trying to remain the man I have become while I was at war.

Glossary of Terms and Abbreviations

ACC	Acute care clinic
AFN	Armed Forces Network
ASMC	Area support medical company
BAMC	Brooke Army Medical Center, Ft. Sam Houston, TX
BIAP	Baghdad International Airport
CME	Continuing Medical Education
CSH	Combat support hospital
DCCS	Deputy commander for clinical services or senior physician in charge
DFAC	Dining facility
ECU	Environmental control units
EMT	Emergency medical treatment or emergency medical technician
EPW	Enemy prisoner of war
ER	Emergency room
FLB	Forward logistics base
HVD	High value detainee
ICU	Intensive care unit
ID	Infantry division
IED	Improvised explosive device
LSA	Life support area or living quarters
MASCAL	Mass casualty, usually mentioned as an exercise
MASH	Mobile Army Surgical Hospital
Med Bde	Medical Brigade
MOPP	Mission oriented protective posture or chemical suits
MP	Military police
MRE	Meals ready to eat
MWR	Morale, welfare and recreation
OIF	Operation Iraqi Freedom
OR	Operating room
PCS	Permanent change of station or moving within the military

PLX	Pharmacy, lab and x-ray
PX	Post Exchange or shopping center
RPG	Rocket-propelled grenade
S3	Staff officer for operations or planning
S4	Staff officer for logistics or supply
TOA	Transfer of authority
TOC	Tactical operations center or command post
TDY	Temporary duty
WAMC	Womack Army Medical Center, Ft. Bragg, NC
WBAMC	William Beaumont Army Medical Center, Ft. Bliss, TX
WRAMC	Walter Reed Army Medical Center, Washington, D.C.

Photographs / 9 Mar 03–15 Feb 04

The 28th CSH waits to board the planes at Green Ramp, Pope Air Force Base, North Carolina.

The Forward Unit receives a send-off by the remaining members as we leave Kuwait.

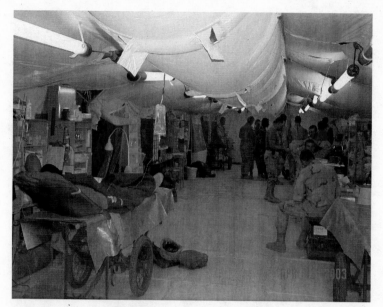

The EMT section at Dogwood

Physicians and staff surround a patient in the EMT section, Dogwood.

The 28th CSH-Dogwood medical staff, LTC Hodges is third from the left, wearing sunglasses.

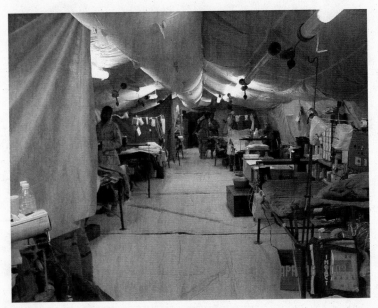

One of the Intensive Care Units at Dogwood

Aerial view of 28th CSH-Dogwood

Raising tents as we set-up our hospital at FLB Dogwood

A mural of Saddam Hussain in Tallil, Iraq

Crossing through the Karbala Gap

My cot and living space in Tikrit

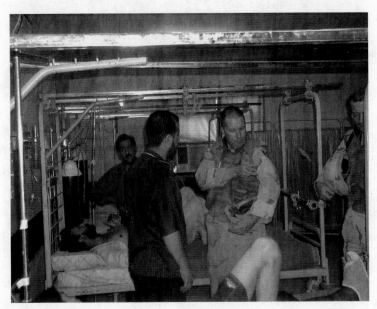

LTC Hodges discussing patient care at one of the Iraqi hospitals in Tikrit

OLD NAVY
AN AMERICAN TRADITION
2003

06/29/20

Hodges Family July

07/01/20

The July 4th photo my wife created as part of our annual tradition. It was published in our local paper, *The Fayetteville Observer*.

12/20/2003

Christmas decorations in the chapel in Tikrit

01/07/2004

Tikrit housing trailer that arrived in December 2003

LTC Hodges standing by the tents of 28th CSH-Tikrit

The men's latrine at Dogwood, this was the first version. Later we had individual units.

Being avid NASCAR fans, MAJ William Dixon (L) and LTC Hodges (R), celebrate their favorite track with a sign.

Watching medevac helicopters landing from the roof at 28th csh-Ibn Sina

Aerial view of 28th csh-Tikrit

Daddy's Home!

TATE PUBLISHING *& Enterprises*

Tate Publishing is committed to excellence in the publishing industry. Our staff of highly trained professionals, including editors, graphic designers, and marketing personnel, work together to produce the very finest books available. The company reflects the philosophy established by the founders, based on Psalms 68:11,

"THE LORD GAVE THE WORD AND GREAT WAS THE COMPANY OF THOSE WHO PUBLISHED IT."

If you would like further information, please call
1.888.361.9473
or visit our website
www.tatepublishing.com

TATE PUBLISHING *& Enterprises*, LLC
127 E. Trade Center Terrace
Mustang, Oklahoma 73064 USA